Modern Critical Interpretations

# William Shakespeare's Macbeth

# Modern Critical Interpretations

*These and other titles in preparation*

# William Shakespeare's
# Macbeth

*Edited and with an introduction by*

Harold Bloom
*Sterling Professor of the Humanities*
*Yale University*

*Chelsea House Publishers*

NEW YORK ◇ PHILADELPHIA

Printed and bound in the United States of America

10   9

∞ The paper used in this publication meets the minimum
requirements of the American National Standard for Permanence
of Paper for Printed Library Materials, Z39.48-1984.

Library of Congress Cataloging-in-Publication Data
    William Shakespeare's Macbeth
    (Modern critical interpretations)
    Bibliography: p.
    Includes index.
    1. Shakespeare, William, 1564–1616. Macbeth.
I. Bloom, Harold II. Series.
PR2823.W48   1987       822.3′3       86-33447
ISBN 0–87754–930–3

# Contents

# Editor's Note

This book gathers together what I judge to be a representative selection of the most useful criticism devoted to Shakespeare's *Macbeth*. The critical essays are reprinted here in the chronological order of their original publication. I am grateful to David Parker for his assistance in editing this volume.

My introduction centers upon the fearful paradox that Macbeth's overwhelming interest for us increases even as he empties his cosmos out more and more until it is a Gnostic wasteland. The chronological sequence of criticism begins with Harold Goddard's powerful study of just how "Macbeth *has betrayed himself* to the equivocal and the illusory." L. C. Knights follows with his classic discussion of the play's portrayal of the lust for power.

The drama's imagery of banqueting is closely examined by Maynard Mack, Jr., after which Howard Felperin applies Paul de Man's dialectic of literary modernity to the determination of *Macbeth*'s relation to dramatic tradition. Harry Levin sharply analyzes two crucial scenes from the play, so as to throw illuminating sidelights upon Macbeth as hero-villain.

This volume concludes with Robert N. Watson's full-scale Gnostic exegesis of *Macbeth*, which contrasts with my own Oedipal account of the hero-villain's nihilistic nature in my introduction.

# Introduction

Critics remark endlessly about two aspects of *Macbeth,* its obsession with "time," and its invariable recourse to metaphors of the stage, almost on the scale of *Hamlet. Macbeth,* my personal favorite among Shakespeare's dramas, always has seemed to me to be set in a Gnostic cosmos, though certainly Shakespeare's own vision is by no means Gnostic in spirit. Gnosticism always manifests a great horror of time, since time will show that one is nothing in oneself, and that one's ambition to be everything in oneself is only an imitation of the Demiurge, the maker of this ruined world.

Why does Shakespeare give us the theatrical trope throughout *Macbeth,* in a universe that is the *kenoma,* the cosmological emptiness of the Gnostic seers? In *Hamlet,* the trope is appropriate, since Claudius governs a play-act kingdom. Clearly, we confront a more desperate theatricality in *Macbeth,* where the cosmos, and not just the kingdom, is an apocalyptic stage, even as it is in *King Lear.* Macbeth's obsession with time is the actor's obsession, and the director's, rather than the poet-playwright's. It is the fear of saying the wrong thing at the wrong time, thus ruining the illusion, which is that one is anything at all.

What always remains troublingly sympathetic about Macbeth is partly that he represents our own Oedipal ambitions, and partly that his opposition to true nature *is* Faustian. Brutally murderous, Macbeth nevertheless is profoundly and engagingly imaginative. He is a visionary Jacobean hero-villain, but unlike Richard III, Iago, and Edmund, and unlike the hero-villains of Webster and Tourneur (Bosola, Flamineo, Ludovico, Vindice), Macbeth takes no pride or pleasure in limning his night-piece and finding it his best. Partly that is because he does not and cannot limn it wholly by himself anyway. Both the supernatural and the natural play a very large part—the witches throughout, and the legitimately natural, almost genealogical revenge of Birnam Wood coming to Dunsinane.

These interventions, demonic and retributive, mean that Macbeth never can get anything quite right, and he is always too cursed with imagination not to know it. Macbeth, far from being the author of that greatest of all night-pieces, *Macbeth,* is merely the object of the drama's force, so much a part of its terrible nature that he needs to augment his crimes steadily just so as to prolong himself in time.

Macbeth's originality as a representation is what makes him so shockingly more interesting than anyone else in the play. This is not just to repeat the commonsense notion that literary evil is much more fascinating than literary good; Lady Macbeth after all is considerably less absorbing for us than her husband is. Nor is it even the consequence of what Howard Felperin terms Macbeth's "literary modernity," his constant re-invention of his own nature, his inability to take that nature for granted. Why are the other male characters in *Macbeth* so gray, so difficult to distinguish from one another in character or personality? Shakespeare wastes little labor in portraying even Duncan and Banquo, let alone Macduff, Malcolm, and Donalbain. As for Lennox, Rosse, Menteth, Angus, Cathness—you could not tell these players apart even if a scorecard were provided. The dramatist grants high individuality only to Macbeth, and by doing so makes us confront what it is that we find so attractive in this very bloody villain.

I surmise that Macbeth is so dreadfully interesting because it is his intense *inwardness* that always goes bad, and indeed keeps getting worse down to the very end. His is an inversion of that biblical dualism set forth by Jeremiah the prophet, in which we are taught the injustice of outwardness and the potential morality of our inwardness, which demands justice against the outside world. As a Shakespearean representation, Macbeth empties out inwardness without making it any less interesting; we cannot understand either his nihilism or his imaginative force if we rely upon a superior moral stance in relation to him. That moral stance is not available to us, not just because our own ambitions are perpetually murderous, but primarily because we *are* interesting to ourselves for precisely the reasons that Macbeth is interesting to us. And what makes us interesting to ourselves is that we have learned to see ourselves as we see Macbeth.

He has taught us that we are more interesting to ourselves than others can be precisely because their inwardness is not available to us. If cognitively we have learned disinterestedness from Hamlet, or learned that we can love only those who do not seem to need our love, then cognitively we have learned a dangerously attractive solipsism from Macbeth. Hamlet and Falstaff are not solipsists, for wit demands both other selves and a world external to the self. Macbeth is neither a wit nor a Counter-Machiavel, like Hamlet and Falstaff, nor a Machiavel, like Edmund and Iago. He neither writes with words nor with the other characters. He simply murders what is outward to himself, and at the end is not even certain that Lady Macbeth was not outward to himself. He remains so original a representation of the simultaneous necessity and disaster of a constantly augmenting inwardness that we have not caught up with him yet. Perhaps his greatest horror for us is his brooding conviction that there is sense in everything, which means that he is totally overdetermined even as he tries so murderously to make himself into something new.

## II

*Macbeth,* even in the somewhat uncertain form that we have it, is a ruthlessly economical drama, marked by a continuous eloquence astonishing even for Shakespeare. It cannot be an accident that it is the last of the four supreme tragedies, following *Hamlet, Othello,* and *Lear.* Shakespeare surpasses even those plays here in maintaining a continuous pitch of tragic intensity, in making everything overwhelmingly dark with meaning. Early on, Macbeth states the ethos of his drama:

> My thought, whose murther yet is but fantastical,
> Shakes so my single state of man that function
> Is smother'd in surmise, and nothing is
> But what is not.

Murder is the center, and will not cease to perplex Macbeth, for whom its ontological status, as it were, has been twisted askew:

> The time has been,
> That when the brains were out, the man would die,
> And there an end; but now they rise again
> With twenty mortal murthers on their crowns,

And push us from our stools. This is more strange
Than such a murther is.

Everything that Macbeth speaks in the course of the drama leads into its most famous and most powerful speech, as fierce a Gnostic declaration as exists in our language:

To-morrow, and to-morrow, and to-morrow,
Creeps in this petty pace from day to day,
To the last syllable of recorded time;
And all our yesterdays have lighted fools
The way to dusty death. Out, out, brief candle!
Life's but a walking shadow, a poor player,
That struts and frets his hour upon the stage,
And then is heard no more. It is a tale
Told by an idiot, full of sound and fury,
Signifying nothing.

The dramatist, according to Macbeth, is the Demiurge, who destroys all meaning whatsoever. But his nihilistic play, featuring life as hero-villain, is so badly acted in its most crucial part that the petty pace of fallen time is only accentuated. Macbeth therefore ends in total consciousness that he has been thrown into the cosmological emptiness:

I gin to be a-weary of the sun,
And wish th' estate o' th' world were now undone.

Mysticism, according to an ancient formulation, fails and then becomes apocalyptic. The apocalyptic fails, and then becomes Gnosticism. Gnosticism, having no hopes for or in this life, necessarily cannot fail. Macbeth, at the close, cannot fail, because he has murdered all hope and all meaning. What he has not murdered is only interest, our interest, our own deep investment in our own inwardness, at all costs, at every cost. Bloody tyrant though he be, Macbeth remains the unsurpassed representation of imagination gone beyond limits, into the abyss of our emptiness.

# Macbeth

## Harold C. Goddard

> *Men are probably nearer to the essential truth in their superstitions than in their science.*
>
> HENRY DAVID THOREAU

In spite of the intimate links between *Hamlet* and *Othello*, if there were no external evidence to the contrary a case could be made for the view that *Macbeth* was the tragedy to come next after *Hamlet*, just as a case can be made for the view that *Macbeth* preceded rather than followed *King Lear*. In the former instance I have conformed to the nearly unanimous opinion of scholars. In the latter, more doubtful one I reverse the more generally accepted sequence and take up *Macbeth* before *King Lear*.

*Macbeth* and *King Lear* were so nearly contemporary that the question of their exact dates is not of overwhelming importance. It is psychological development, not chronology, that counts. And the two are not the same. We frequently go back in going forward. There are eddies in the stream. Ascent and descent are not continuous. We may go down temporarily in climbing a mountain. The child often resembles a grandparent more than he does either father or mother, and there is a similar alternation of generations in the world of art. Because one work is full of echoes of another does not prove that it must have immediately succeeded it. The likeness of *Macbeth* to *Hamlet* is no obstacle to the belief that *Othello* came be-

From *The Meaning of Shakespeare.* © 1951 by the University of Chicago. The University of Chicago Press, 1951.

tween them, nor that of *King Lear* to *Othello* to the possibility that *Macbeth* may have intervened.

But somehow the idea that *King Lear* was written before *Macbeth* seems to involve more than this. It is a bit like thinking that *The Brothers Karamazov* was written before *Crime and Punishment*. The analogy is not a casual one. *Macbeth*, like *Crime and Punishment*, is a study of evil through a study of murder. Each is its author's most rapid, concentrated, terrific, and possibly sublime work. Each is a prolonged nightmare lifted into the realm of art. *King Lear* and *The Brothers Karamazov* are also studies of evil; but if they sound no lower depths, they do climb to greater heights than *Macbeth* and *Crime and Punishment*. All four fight through again the old war between light and darkness. But in *Macbeth* and *Crime and Punishment* we have "night's predominance," as Shakespeare phrases it, and the light is that of a star or two in the blackness, while in *King Lear* and *The Brothers Karamazov* the stars are morning stars and there is dawn on the horizon. I know how preposterous this will sound to those who consider *King Lear* the pessimistic masterpiece of the ages.

## II

If it be true that all art aspires to the state of music, the opening of *Macbeth* approximates perfection. The contention of the elements and the battles of men are the themes of the witches' colloquy. But their lines are more overture than scene, and the drama has a second opening in the account given by the wounded Sergeant of Macbeth's conquest of the rebels. The passage is like a smear of blood across the first page of the play. The double opening defines precisely what we are to expect: a work dedicated not to the supernatural nor to blood but to the relation between the two. (The modern reader who is afraid of the word "supernatural" may substitute "unconscious.") Passion means originally the capacity to be affected by external agents. In this sense *Macbeth* is a play about human passion.

It is significant that the witches choose for their fatal encounter with Macbeth not the hour of battle but the moment

> When the hurlyburly's done.

War plows the soil. Who wins is not what counts. It is what seeds are planted

> When the battle's lost and won

that determines the future. Only that future can determine who did win. The phrase might well be written lost-and-won. Already in *Much Ado about Nothing* and *All's Well That Ends Well* (not to mention the Histories) Shakespeare had touched on the aftereffects of war on character. Men who have been valiant on the battlefield can come home to act like cads or criminals in time of peace.

The account of Macbeth's disemboweling of Macdonwald is one of the goriest things in Shakespeare. "Fie, savage, fie!" we are tempted to cry, remembering Hector. But

> O valiant cousin! worthy gentleman!

is the way Duncan greets the bloody story. As a concordance will show, Bernard Shaw himself takes no greater delight than the gentle Shakespeare in using the word "gentleman" with devastating sarcasm.

> Let each man render me his bloody hand
> 
> . . . . . . . . . . . . . . . . . . . .
> 
> Gentlemen all,

says Antony to the assassins of Caesar, conscious of his irony as Duncan was not.

> this dead butcher and his fiend-like queen

is the way Malcolm, with the finality of an epitaph, sums up this worthy gentleman and his wife in the last speech of the play. It is fitting that it should open with an example of his butchery. Macbeth, murderer of Duncan, and Macbeth, tyrant of Scotland, are implicit in Macbeth, slaughterer of Macdonwald. Yet there was a time, we feel, when Macbeth may have been gentle.

The opening scene and the closing act of *Macbeth* are given to war; the rest of the first act and the second to murder; the third and fourth to tyranny—with further murder. The play leaves us with the feeling that offensive war, crime, and tyranny are merely different faces of the same monster. Tyranny is just war catching its breath. Under it the preponderance of power is so markedly on one side that open violence is no longer necessary. The Enemy is now the subjects. If the fragmentary passages describing Scotland under Macbeth are assembled, they read like a documented account of life in the countries subjugated by the "strong" men of the twentieth century. With its remote setting and ancient superstitions, *Macbeth* to a superficial mind may seem dated. On the contrary few of Shakespeare's plays speak more directly to our time.

III

How did Shakespeare have the audacity to center a tragedy around a murderer and tyrant, a man so different in his appeal to our sympathies from a Romeo, a Brutus, or a Hamlet? He had done something of the sort before in *Richard III,* but Richard is more nearly a melodramatic and theatrical than a strictly tragic success. Doubts remain in many minds whether such a creature could ever have existed. But Macbeth is at bottom any man of noble intentions who gives way to his appetites. And who at one time or another has not been that man? Who, looking back over his life, cannot perceive some moral catastrophe that he escaped by inches? Or did not escape. *Macbeth* reveals how close we who thought ourselves safe may be to the precipice. Few readers, however, feel any such kinship with Macbeth as they do with Hamlet. We do not expect to be tempted to murder; but we do know what it is to have a divided soul. Yet Hamlet and Macbeth are imaginative brothers. The difference is that Macbeth begins more or less where Hamlet left off.

> Now might I do it pat, now he is praying,

says the latter, meditating the death of the King,

> And now I'll do 't. And so he goes to heaven;
> And so am I reveng'd. *That would be scann'd.*

> Strange things I have in head, that will to hand,
> Which must be acted *ere they may be scann'd,*

says Macbeth, plotting the destruction of the Macduffs [author's italics]. The two couplets seem written to match each other. Yet Hamlet had to go down only a corridor or so from the praying King to commit a deed, the killing of Polonius, of which Macbeth's couplet is a perfect characterization.

> My strange and self-abuse,

says Macbeth, unstrung at the sight of Banquo's ghost,

> Is the initiate fear that wants hard use:
> We are yet but young in deed.

Deeds, he divines, are the only opiates for fears, but their defect as a remedy is the fact that the dose must be increased with an alarming rapidity.

> O, from this time forth,

cried Hamlet, shamed at the sight of the efficient Fortinbras,

> My thoughts be bloody, or be nothing worth!

The Macbeth-in-Hamlet meant *deeds,* but there was enough of the original Hamlet still left in him to keep it "thoughts." But bloody thoughts are the seed of bloody deeds, and Macbeth, with the very accent of the Fortinbras soliloquy, says, without Hamlet's equivocation,

> from this moment
> The very firstlings of my heart shall be
> The firstlings of my hand.

The harvest of this creed is of course a complete atrophy of heart.

> The time has been my senses would have cool'd
> To hear a night-shriek,

he says when that atrophy has overtaken him,

> and my fell of hair
> Would at a dismal treatise rouse and stir
> As life were in't.

That is Macbeth gazing back, as it were, into his Hamletian past ("Angels and ministers of grace defend us!"), quite as Hamlet looks forward into his Macbethian future. In that sense the rest was not silence.

Hamlet is to Macbeth somewhat as the Ghost is to the Witches. Revenge, or ambition, in its inception may have a lofty, even a majestic countenance; but when it has "coupled hell" and become crime, it grows increasingly foul and sordid. We love and admire Hamlet so much at the beginning that we tend to forget that he is as hot-blooded as the earlier Macbeth when he kills Polonius and the King, cold-blooded as the later Macbeth or Iago when he sends Rosencrantz and Guildenstern to death. If in *Othello* we can trace fragments of a divided Hamlet transmigrated into Desdemona and Iago, in *Macbeth* an undivided Hamlet keeps straight onward and downward in Macbeth himself. The murderer of Duncan inherits Hamlet's sensibility, his nervous irritability, his hysterical passion, his extraordinary gifts of visualization and imaginative expression; and under the instigating influence of his wife the "rashness" and "indiscretion" of the later Hamlet are progressively translated into a succession of mad acts.

It is this perhaps that explains the main technical peculiarity of *Macbeth,* its brevity. It is so short that not a few have thought that what has come down to us is just the abbreviated stage version of a much longer play. As it stands, it has no "beginning" in the Aristotelian sense, scarcely even a "middle." It is mostly "end." The hero has already been tempted before the opening of the action. We do not know how long he has been turning the murder over in his mind before he broaches the matter to his wife, in a decisive scene which is recapitulated in half a dozen lines near the end of act 1 and which occurred before Macbeth encountered the Weird Sisters. This is exactly the way Dostoyevski manages it in *Crime and Punishment,* where Raskolnikov is represented as having lain for days on his bed "thinking" before the story actually opens, and we learn only retrospectively of his meeting the previous winter with the officer and student in the tavern who echo his innermost guilty thoughts and consolidate his fatal impulse precisely as the Weird Sisters do Macbeth's. If the novelist abstains from attempting a detailed account of the period when the crime was being incubated, is it any wonder that the dramatist does, especially when he has already accomplished something resembling this seemingly impossible dramatic representation of inaction in the first two acts of *Hamlet?* Why repeat it? When we consider *Macbeth* as a separate work of art, what its author did or didn't do in another work has of course nothing to do with it. But when we consider the plays, and especially the Tragedies, as chapters of a greater whole, it has everything to do with it. What may be a disadvantage, or even a flaw, from the point of view of the man witnessing *Macbeth* for the first time in the theater may be anything but that to a reader of all the Tragedies in order. And the truth of the statement is in no wise diminished if we hold that Shakespeare himself was largely unconscious of the psychic relationship of his plays.

Viewed in the context of his other works, *Macbeth* is Shakespeare's Descent into Hell. And since it is his *Inferno,* it is appropriate that the terrestrial and celestial parts of his universe should figure in it slightly.

Explorations of the underworld have been an unfailing feature of the world's supreme poetry. From the Greek myths and Homer, to go no farther back or further afield, through the Greek dramatists and the theological-religious visions of Dante and Milton, on to the symbolic poems and prophecies of Blake and the psychological-religious novels of Dostoyevski, we meet wide variations on a theme that remains basically the same. All versions of it, we are at last in a position to recognize, are attempts to represent the psychic as distinguished from the physical world. The difference in nomenclature should not blind us to the identity of subject. We could salvage vast tracts of what is held to be the obsolete wisdom of the world if we would recognize that fact. Wisdom does not become obsolete.

## IV

Yet there is a historical criticism which thinks Shakespeare was pandering to the superstitions of his audience in *Macbeth* and following a stage tradition rather than life in his study of the criminal nature. Professor Stoll, for instance, in his *Shakespeare Studies* devotes a long chapter, "The Criminals," to proving that Shakespeare's tragic evildoers are not "the real thing." If we seek the real thing we will find it rather, he says, in what science has discovered about the criminal, and what realistic literature, following in its footsteps, has portrayed, in the last century or two. "Men are neither good nor evil," says Professor Stoll, quoting Balzac. "In Nature," he goes on (no longer quoting), "the good and the bad, the healthy and the degenerate, are inextricably interwoven, are one. It was quite another atmosphere that Shakespeare breathed, an atmosphere charged with the dualism of the Middle Ages and earlier times. Good and evil then were as the poles asunder." "The web of our life is of a mingled yarn, good and ill together"; says Shakespeare, "our virtues would be proud, if our faults whipped them not; and our crimes would despair, if they were not cherished by our virtues." Professor Stoll's idea of the modern attitude exactly, down to the very metaphor! It is a Lord in *All's Well That Ends Well* speaking, but there is *Measure for Measure* with its "write good angel on the devil's horn" to show how completely Shakespeare agreed with him. And not one of his greater plays—including even *King Lear,* in which good and evil are indeed fiercely contrasted—but shows the same. Yet is was "quite another atmosphere that Shakespeare breathed." In that case, he did not make his plays out of the surrounding atmosphere.

Professor Stoll cites numerous near-contemporary examples (in which jockeys, gypsies, horse thieves, and pirates figure) to prove not merely the unrepentant but the carefree mood of the "real" criminal after his crime, in contrast with that of the Elizabethan stage offender. "After the crime they go on a lark, play cards with the family, or take a nap," he tells us. "How shallow and obsequious of us," he continues, "to bow to Shakespeare and almost all the choice and master spirits in drama and fiction up to the present age, in their opinion that though there is joy in our hearts when we engage in works of justice and mercy there is no joy in the heart of the miser as he hoards or in the heart of the murderer as he kills! Do we do good because, despite all, we love it, but they evil because they hate it? We ourselves know better." How almost all the choice and master spirits in drama and fiction up to our own more enlightened age happened to agree in their common blindness to notorious fact in this matter is not explained, but among the more modern and less deluded authorities that are cited against Aeschylus, Shakespeare, and Molière are such men as Sudermann, Pinero, and Henry Arthur Jones. Tolstoy is cited too, but he, as Professor Stoll admits, slipped back into the classic error in *The Power of Darkness*.

However that may be, I see no evidence that Shakespeare was unacquainted with either the lighthearted or the callous type of criminal. Autolycus is as carefree a pickpocket as anyone could ask for. Pistol, granted the caricature in his case, is admirably true to the supposedly "modern" criminal type; while it would be hard in all the literature of the nineteenth and twentieth centuries to match the self-possessed Barnardine in *Measure for Measure*, who, as we have seen, coolly upsets all plans for his execution by simply refusing to accommodate the prison authorities. And if anyone thinks these instances edge too near to farce, there are John of Lancaster, who commits his supreme treachery without an inkling, apparently, of its depravity, and Cloten, who goes to his most unspeakable crime in precisely the spirit which Professor Stoll so exhaustively documents. Iago says his plotting gives him so much pleasure that he forgets the passage of time, and even Hamlet—Iago-Hamlet—murders Polonius almost casually, refers to his corpse as if it were a sack of meal, and later comes home from his callous dispatch to death of his old school-fellows, Rosencrantz and Guildenstern, to exchange quibbles, however gravely, with the gravediggers—without a single apparent touch of remorse. The Duke of Cornwall, it is plainly hinted, did not intend to let his turning of the aged King Lear into the storm interfere in the slightest degree with a comfortable evening indoors at home. And the list could easily be extended. The discovery that criminals—many of them—can be carefree before, during, and after the crime may be one of the glories of scientific criminology but it would have been no news to Shakespeare.

Professor Stoll's modern instances are unassailable as far as they go, but what he fails to note is exactly what Shakespeare is so careful to observe: that there are criminals and criminals. As usual, he will not be seduced into too easy generalization or classification, and, instead of presenting us with a "criminal type," gives us every variety of offender against the law. His hired assassins, even when they speak only a few lines, are individualized, and, when there are several of them together, one is often of the carefree sort while one will hesitate and tremble. Professor Stoll's admission in passing that in *comedy* the earlier drama approximates what he calls the facts about the criminal nature is fatal to his argument. For in that case the practice in tragedy of Shakespeare and the other choice and master spirits was obviously not the result of ignorance but of something distinctive about the *tragic* criminal.

What that something is, the difference between Macbeth and Lady Macbeth makes plain, for the husband, not the wife, is the truly tragic figure, and the play is rightly entitled *Macbeth,* not *The Macbeths*. Professor Stoll's own criminological data suggest just this distinction. He quotes penological authorities to show that the sleep of criminals is not disturbed by uneasy dreams and that signs of repentance, remorse, or despair are seldom to be detected in them. In one group of four hundred murderers such signs were found in only three, and in another group of seven hundred criminals only 3.4 percent "showed signs of repentance or appeared at all moved in recounting their misdeeds." That that exceptional 3.4 percent were specimens of what Nietzsche calls the "pale criminal" and included probably the only ones capable of exciting tragic interest Professor Stoll does *not* go on to say. Imaginative literature is not criminology, and, except incidentally or for purposes of contrast, has no interest in portraying primitive, brutal, or moronic types. When rich or noble natures display atavistic traits or slip back into atavistic conduct, as do Hamlet and Othello, those traits begin to assume tragic interest, for tragedy has to do with men possessing the capacity to become gods who, momentarily at least, become devils. The normal man has little in common with these murderers of Professor Stoll's who slay their victims as unconcernedly as an old hand in a slaughterhouse kills cattle. But the normal man, in his lesser degree, *is* Orestes, Macbeth, and Raskolnikov. Such characters tell us, not how the ordinary run of criminals react, but how Aeschylus and Shakespeare and Dostoyevski would have felt, if they had themselves fallen into crime. They are the 3 percent of the 3 percent.

Professor Stoll derides especially the idea that criminals are obsessed with the horror of their deeds before they commit them: "Who sins thus, against the grain?" Or immediately after: "Instead of hearing, like the Scottish thane and the English king, ominous voices," real criminals, he tells us, are likely, after a murder, to fall asleep on the spot, or at least to sleep better afterward. And he cites Raskolnikov in *Crime and Punishment* as one of his examples—a most unfortunate one for his argument, for if ever a man was depicted as both sinning against the grain and being punished *instantly* for his deed it is Raskolnikov. Turn to the text. In the first chapter the murderer-to-be characterizes the crime he is to commit—which he can bring himself to refer to only as *that*—as hideous, loathsome, filthy, and disgusting, two of the four adjectives being identically Macbeth's. ("Temptations," says Professor Stoll, "are not hideous but beautiful." If he had said "fascinating," we could have agreed.) Yet Raskolnikov goes out to do the deed drawn by a power over which he *now* has no control—just as Macbeth was marshaled by the air-drawn dagger. And when does Dostoyevski show his murderer sleeping "better" after the murder? He goes home from it to one fearful nightmare after another, to sleep

> In the affliction of these terrible dreams
> That shake us nightly,

and to say, in effect, exactly as Shakespeare makes Macbeth say:

> Better be with the dead,
> Whom we, to gain our peace, have sent to peace,
> Than on the torture of the mind to lie
> In restless ecstasy.

"Crime and punishment," says Emerson, "grow out of one stem. . . . All infractions of love and equity in our social relations are speedily punished. They are punished by fear. . . . Commit a crime, and the earth is made of glass. Commit a crime, and it seems as if a coat of snow fell on the ground, such as reveals in the woods the track of every partridge and fox and squirrel and mole." Was Emerson, too, an Elizabethan? On the contrary, like Shakespeare and Dostoyevski, he was not a "fool of time."

Shakespeare's play and Dostoyevski's novel are both dedicated to the proof of Emerson's proposition. Different as are the literary traditions from which they stem, opposite in many respects as are the techniques of drama and fiction, point by point, detail by detail, Shakespeare's and Dostoyevski's treatments of the criminal heart and mind correspond. It is one of the most impressive analogies in all literature: an overwhelming demonstration that genius is independent of time. "Psychologically he was for the age correct," says Professor Stoll of Shakespeare. As if the soul altered from age to age, and was busy, about A.D. 1600, conforming to the conventions of the Elizabethan stage! "In that day when men still believed in diabolical possession," he begins. As if Job and Aeschylus, Dante and the Gospels were obsolete! The fact that the ignorant of all ages have believed in diabolical possession in a superstitious sense is no reason for blinding our eyes to the fact that the imaginative geniuses of all ages have also believed in it in another and profounder sense. And so, too, of the prodigies in the sky and elsewhere that accompany murder in Shakespeare and the Elizabethan drama. "Through it all," says Professor Stoll, "runs the notion that the moment of sin and the manner of the sinner are something prodigious and beyond the bounds of nature, as indeed they appear to be in the person of many a famous actor who saws the air in old paintings and prints." Professor Stoll in that sentence comes perilously close to saying that the moment of sin is *not* prodigious. The possibility that these supposedly astronomical and other portents may be psychical rather than physical phenomena—waking nightmares projected on shapes of the natural world that seem expressly molded to receive them—he does not appear to have taken into account. (Not to suggest thereby that they are just subjective.)

## V

Deeds of violence that come exclusively out of the brute in man have no tragic significance and take their place in human memory with the convulsions of nature and the struggle to survive of the lower orders of life. But when a man of imagination—by which I mean a man in whom the image of God is distinct—stoops to crime, instantly transcendental powers rush to the scene as if fearful lest this single deed shift the moral center of gravity of the universe, as a finger may tip an immense boulder that is in delicate equilibrium. Macbeth and Lady Macbeth (as she was at the outset) seem created to stress this distinction. "A little water clears us of this deed," is her reaction to the murder of Duncan.

> Will all great Neptune's ocean wash this blood
> Clean from my hand? No, this my hand will rather
> The multitudinous seas incarnadine,
> Making the green one red,

is his. One wonders whether the supremacy of the moral imagination over the material universe was ever more tremendously expressed than in those four lines. In them, space is, as it were, forever put in its place. When Lady Macbeth, in the end, attains the same insight that is Macbeth's instantly—"all the perfumes of Arabia will not sweeten this little hand"—she does not pass, it is to be noted, to the second part of the generalization. It is this defect in imagination that makes her, if a more pathetic, a less tragic figure than her husband.

The medieval mind, in the tradition of mythology, represented the tragic conflict, which our irreligious age is likely to think of as just a strife between opposing impulses, as a struggle between devils and angels for the possession of man's soul. Devils and angels are out of fashion. But it is not the nomenclature that counts, and the soundness of the ancient conception is being confirmed, under another terminology, in the researches of psychology into the unconscious mind.

Now the unconscious, whatever else or more it may be, is an accumulation of the human and prehuman psychic tendencies of life on the planet, and the unconscious of any individual is a reservoir that contains latently the experience of all his ancestors. This potential inheritance is naturally an inextricable mixture of good and evil. Hence whenever the threshold of consciousness is sufficiently lowered to permit an influx of the unconscious, a terrific tension arises between forces pulling the individual in different or opposite directions. Samuel Butler has given classic expression to this struggle in *Life and Habit:*

It is one against legion when a creature tries to differ from his own past selves. He must yield or die if he wants to differ widely, so as to lack natural instincts, such as hunger or thirst, or not to gratify them. . . . His past selves are living in unruly hordes within him at this moment and overmastering him. "Do this, this, this, which we too have done, and found our profit in it," cry the souls of his forefathers within him. Faint are the far ones, coming and going as the sound of bells wafted on to a high mountain; loud and clear are the near ones, urgent as an alarm of fire. "Withhold," cry some. "Go on boldly," cry others. "Me, me, me, revert hitherward, my descendant," shouts one as it were from some high vantage-ground over the heads of the clamorous multitude. "Nay, but me, me, me," echoes another; and our former selves fight within us and wrangle for our possession. Have we not here what is commonly called an *internal tumult,* when dead pleasures and pains tug within us hither and thither? Then may the battle be decided by what people are pleased to call our own experience. Our own indeed!

This passage makes clear why an unmediated polarity is a distinguishing mark of the unconscious and suggests a biological reason for the Delphic character of all true oracles. Every sentence, declares Thoreau, has two sides: "One faces the world, but the other is infinite and confronts the gods." An oracular utterance is merely an extreme form of such a sentence, an incarnation in microcosmic form of the duality Butler depicts. In choosing between its worldly or infernal and its unworldly or celestial meaning, the individual without realizing it recruits an army, the good or bad impulses and acts of millions who have gone before him. Dreams too—many of them —have this ambiguous character and without violence to their imagery can often be taken in contradictory senses. And tragic irony always can. But so hidden may be the second meaning that it requires the future to reveal it, as it may take a second or several readings to uncover it in the printed play.

## VI

From end to end, *Macbeth* is packed with these Delphic effects as is no other work of Shakespeare's: words, acts, and situations which may be interpreted or taken in two ways at the peril of the chooser and which in the aggregate produce an overwhelming conviction that behind the visible world lies another world, immeasurably wider and deeper, on its relation to which human destiny turns. As a face now reveals and now conceals the life behind it, so the visible world now hides this other world as does a wall, now opens on it as does a door. In either case it is *there*—there not as a matter of philosophical speculation or of theological tradition or hypothesis, but there as a matter of psychic fact.

Scholars who dismiss the supernatural elements in *Macbeth* as stage convention or condescension to popular superstition stamp themselves as hopelessly insensitive not merely to poetry but to sincerity. Not only the plot and characters of the play, which are up to a certain point the author's inventions, but its music, imagery, and atmosphere—effects only partly under his conscious control—unite in giving the impression of mighty and inscrutable forces behind human life. Only one convinced of the reality of these forces could conceivably have imparted such an overwhelming sense of their presence. Neither could a mere stage contrivance have exercised the influence *Macbeth* has over the imaginations of later poets: Milton, Blake, the Keats of *Hyperion*, Emily Brontë, to name no others. Each sees the poet's vocation, as Shakespeare did in *Macbeth*, as an attempt to reclaim a dark region of the soul. "Shine inward," is the blind Milton's prayer to Celestial Light, ". . . there plant eyes." "To open the immortal Eyes of Man inwards," says Blake, is his great task. "To see as a god sees," cries Keats,

> and take the depth
> Of things as nimbly as the outward eye
> Can size and shape pervade.

*Macbeth* is a milestone in man's exploration of precisely this "depth of things" which our age calls the unconscious. The very phrase "depth psychology" has been used to differentiate the psychology of the unconscious from shallower attempts to understand the mind.

The more obviously Janus-like passages in *Macbeth*, where the surface meaning is contradicted from below, have often been pointed out. The double intention of the three prophecies concerning the invulnerability of Macduff, Birnam Wood, and the progeny of Banquo no one could miss. These, to be sure, have their theatrical aspect. But they have universal undertones and overtones. Many examples of dramatic irony in the play, too, are familiar: Macbeth's "Fail not our feast," with Banquo's prophetic reply, "My lord, I will not"; the entrance of Macbeth the moment after Duncan has asserted that treachery cannot be read in the face; the appearance of Lady Macbeth just as Macbeth is lamenting his lack of a spur to the murder; Macbeth's words to the murderer outside the window concerning the blood of Banquo that stains his face:

'Tis better thee without than he within,

a line that fairly gleams and undulates with protean meanings. Following one another in uninterrupted succession these things ultimately produce the conviction that there is something deep in life with power to reverse all its surface indications, as if its undercurrent set in just the opposite direction from the movement on its surface.

Take the famous knocking in the scene following the murder of Duncan.

I hear a knocking
At the south entry,

says Lady Macbeth. "Here's a knocking, indeed!" exclaims the Porter (who has been carousing till the second cock) and goes on to fancy himself the porter of hell gate.

Whence is that knocking?
How is 't with me, when every noise appalls me?

cries Macbeth. It is the same knocking—Macduff and Lennox come to arouse the Porter at the gate—but the sound might just as well be in three separate universes for all it has in common to the three listeners. Lady Macbeth hears it with her senses only; the Porter (dragged out of a dream perhaps) with a slightly drunken comic fancy; Macbeth with the tragic imagination. The sensitive reader hears it differently with each. How shall the man in the theater hear it? Here is a poetical effect beyond the capacity of the stage.

And yet it might be managed better there than it generally is. At such performances of the play at least as I remember, the knocking is heard from the first as a clearly audible noise. This is an obvious mistake. What Macbeth hears is not Macduff and Lennox trying to awaken the Porter, but all the powers of hell and heaven knocking simultaneously at his heart. If the auditor is to feel it with Macbeth, he must hear it with him. His ear and heart, that is, must detect it before his mind. He must hear the sound in Macbeth's listening attitude, in the awe on his face, before the physical sound reaches his ear. He, like Macbeth, must be in doubt as to whether he has heard or only imagined. And so the stage sound should begin below the auditory threshold and mount in a gradual crescendo until it becomes indubitably the pounding at the gate, which, with the dissipation of doubt, brings Macbeth back to earth.

> Wake Duncan with thy knocking! I would thou couldst!

He is at the gate of hell indeed. But still outside. Repentance is yet possible. The cue for the Porter's speech, which follows immediately, is as perfect as if it had been given by thought-transference. And yet the authenticity of the Porter scene has been doubted!

"Is the king stirring, worthy thane?" Macduff inquires when the gate has finally been opened and after Macbeth has returned. "Not yet," replies Macbeth, and what a shudder the future reads into those two words!

"This is the door," says Macbeth. Four words, this time, instead of two, and as ordinary ones as there are in the language. Yet, as Macbeth utters them, they seem whispered back at him in a voice no longer his own, from the very bottom of the universe. How shall an actor get this effect? He cannot. It transcends the theater as certainly as it does not transcend the imagination of the sensitive reader.

Does Lady Macbeth faint, or only pretend to faint, following the discovery of the murder? The point has been much debated. Everything she says or does in this scene is necessarily pretense. She is compelled by the situation to ape the symptoms of fear. But the acting by her body of an assumed fear is the surest way of opening a channel to the genuine fear she is trying to hide. As in the case of Hamlet's antic disposition, the counterfeit on the surface elicits the true from below.

> I will not do 't,

cries Coriolanus when his mother begs him to go through the motions of obeisance to the people,

> Lest I surcease to honour mine own truth,
> And by my body's action teach my mind
> A most inherent baseness.

The psychology here is the same, except that Lady Macbeth does what Coriolanus declares he will not do. Feinting becomes fainting. By sheer willpower (plus a stimulant) Lady Macbeth has held the unconscious out. Now its inundation begins. The end is the sleep-walking scene—and suicide.

At the beginning of the third act Macbeth plans the murder of Banquo. He tries to convince the two cutthroats he has picked for the deed that their ill fortunes in the past were not due to him, as they thought, but to Banquo. His mind is so confused, however, that not only can he not keep track of the passage of time ("Was it not yesterday we spoke together?"), but he mixes hopelessly these men's supposed grievances against Banquo in the past with his own fears of him at present and in the future:

> Are you so gospell'd
> To pray for this good man and *for his issue,*
> Whose heavy hand hath bow'd you to the grave
> *And beggar'd yours for ever?*
>                                    [author's italics]

It is the descendants of Banquo, not the children of the murderers, he is worrying over. And so of the fierce passage about the dogs that follows. Again, it is of himself, not of them, he is speaking, unawares.

> What beast was 't, then,
> That made you break this enterprise to me?

Lady Macbeth had asked long before. At last Macbeth realizes that he is indeed slipping below even "the worst rank of manhood" to a bestial level of "demi-wolves" and "hounds." Of insects, even! as the most horrifying, and yet pathetic, line in the play reveals in the next scene:

> O, full of scorpions is my mind, dear wife!

And so, when he cries to the two he is suborning, "Your spirits shine through you," we know the spirits he glimpses behind them are the same "black agents" to which he has sold himself. Indeed, so closely does he identify himself with these men and the deed they are to commit for him that he tells them no less than four times in a dozen lines that he will be with them presently again: "I will advise you";

"[I will] acquaint you"; "I'll come to you anon"; "I'll call upon you straight."

As the third scene of the third act opens, a third murderer has just joined the other two where they wait at twilight to waylay the unsuspecting Banquo and Fleance. The next twenty-two lines make one of the most eerie passages in Shakespeare. Who is this Third Murderer? Macbeth himself? As all students of the play know, this explanation of the mystery was suggested long ago, and the idea gains a certain plausibility when we notice that Macbeth has pre-pared what might well serve as an alibi to cover a secret absence from the palace.

> Let every man be master of his time
> Till seven at night,

he declares to his lords, just after Banquo leaves for his ride,

> to make society
> The sweeter welcome, we will keep ourself
> Till supper-time alone; while then, God be with you!

and the point has added force when we recall that Portia (Bassanio's Portia) and Imogen covered absences from home that they did not wish noted, in just the same way. How easily, too, Macbeth could have hidden his identity—with darkness and fear to help him further to disguise disguise.

> Come, seeling night,
> Scarf up the tender eye of pitiful day,
> And with thy bloody and invisible hand
> Cancel and tear to pieces that great bond
> Which keeps me pale!

"That great bond" is generally taken as referring to the promise of the Weird Sisters to Banquo, but it might also at the same time refer to the great bond of light which by day holds all good things in harmony but keeps pale the criminal who fears it until night tears it to pieces.

But I do not intend to defend the view that Macbeth was the Third Murderer—or that he was not. I wish rather to call attention to a remarkable fact concerning the response of readers to this ques-tion. Over the years I have called the attention of hundreds to it, most of whom had never heard of it before. It seems to exercise a peculiar fascination and to set even ordinarily casual readers to scanning the text with the minutest attention. And to what conclusion do they come? With a small group no one can predict. But with numbers sufficient to permit the law of averages to apply, the results have an almost scientific consistency. After allowing for a small minority that remains in doubt, about half are convinced that Macbeth was the Third Murderer and the other half are either unconvinced or frankly think the hypothesis farfetched or absurd.

But if the idea that Macbeth was the Third Murderer never entered Shakespeare's head, by what autonomous action of language does the text take on a meaning to the contrary that convinces nearly half of the play's readers? And not only convinces them, but, on the whole, convinces them for the same reasons. That without any basis hundreds should be deluded *in the same way* is unthinkable. But why, then, it will be asked, did not Shakespeare make his intention plain?—a question that reveals a peculiar insensitivity to poetry. What the poet wanted, evidently, was not to make a bald identification of the two men but to produce precisely the effect which as a matter of fact the text does produce on sensitive but unanalytic readers, the feeling, namely, that there is something strange and spectral about the Third Murderer as, unexpected and unannounced, he appears at this remote spot where

> The west yet glimmers with some streaks of day.

Utter darkness is imminent. Now is the time when the last streaks of day in Macbeth's nature are about to fade out forever—and here is the place. Whether he is present or absent in the flesh, it is here and now that he steps through the door above which is written "Abandon all hope, ye who enter." The author must convince us that virtually, if not literally, it is Macbeth who commits the murder. By letting us unconsciously see things simultaneously from two angles, he creates, as sight with two eyes does in the physical world, the true illusion of another dimension, in this case an illusion that annihilates space.

Macbeth's body—who knows?—may have been shut up in his chamber at the palace. But where was the man himself—his ambition, his fear, his straining inner vision, his will? They were so utterly with the hired instruments of that will that we can almost imagine them capable of incarnating themselves in a spectral body and projecting themselves as an apparition to the other two. And who killed Banquo? Is it the cat's paw that pulls the chestnuts from the fire, or he who holds the cat and guides the paw? So here. And we must be made to feel it—whatever we think. It is the poet's duty to bring the spirit of Macbeth to life on the scene. He does.

How he does it is worth pausing a moment to notice—in so far as anything so subtle can be analyzed—for it reveals in miniature the secret of his power over our imaginations throughout the play.

The Third Murderer speaks six times. All but one of his speeches—and that one is but two lines and a half—are brief, one of one word only, and one of two. And every one of these speeches either has something in it to remind us of Macbeth, or might have been spoken by him, or both.

1. When the First Murderer, disturbed, asks who bade him join them, his Delphic answer is:

Macbeth.

2. He is the first to hear the approaching Banquo:

Hark! I hear horses.

The horse, *that on which we ride,* as we have noted elsewhere, is one of the oldest symbols of the unconscious, and that this very symbol is in a highly activated state in Macbeth's mind Shakespeare has been careful to note from his "pity, like a naked new-born babe, striding the blast," and "heaven's cherubin, hors'd upon the sightless couriers of the air" onward. Later, when messengers bring word of Macduff's flight to England, Macbeth's imaginative ear evidently catches the galloping of their horses before it rises above the threshold of consciousness and he translates it into supernatural terms:

MACBETH: Saw you the Weird Sisters?
LENNOX:                    No, my lord.
MACBETH: Came they not by you?
LENNOX:                    No, indeed, my lord.
MACBETH: Infected be the air whereon they ride,
          And damn'd all those that trust them! I did hear
          The galloping of horse: who was 't came by?
LENNOX:  'Tis two or three, my lord, that bring you word
          Macduff is fled to England.

The Weird Sisters could not have been far off, either, when Banquo was murdered. It is interesting, to say the least, that it is the Third

Murderer who first hears the horses. Whoever he is, he is like Macbeth in being sensitive to sound. He and Macbeth, it might be said, hear ear to ear.

3. The Third Murderer's next speech is his longest. To the First Murderer's "His horses go about," he replies:

> Almost a mile; but he does usually—
> So all men do—from hence to th' palace gate
> Make it their walk.

Dashes, in place of the more usual commas, help bring out what is plainly a slip of the tongue on the Third Murderer's part. He has begun to reveal what in the circumstances is a suspicious familiarity with Banquo's habits, when, realizing his mistake, he hurriedly tries to cover it with his plainly parenthetical "so all men do" and his consequently necessary substitution of "their" for "his." But Macbeth does much the same thing just before the murder of Duncan is discovered:

> LENNOX: Goes the king hence today?
> MACBETH:                   He does—he did appoint so.

"He does usually—so all men do." "He does—he did appoint so." Such an echo sounds almost as if it came from the same voice. Only someone like Macbeth in combined impulsiveness and quick repentance of impulsiveness could have spoken the Third Murderer's words.

4. The fourth speech confirms the third:

> 'Tis he.

He is the first to recognize Banquo.

5. "Who did strike out the light?" Who *did?* Is it possible that one of the cutthroats is quite willing to kill a man but balks at the murder of a child? We do not know. But it does not need the King's "Give me some light!" in *Hamlet* or Othello's

> Put out the light, and then put out the light,

to make us aware of a second meaning in this simple question. It was the question that Macbeth must never have ceased to ask himself as he went on down into utter darkness.

6. "There's but one down; the son is fled." The Third Murderer is more perturbed than the others at the escape of Fleance. When at

the beginning of the next scene Macbeth learns from the First Murderer of the death of the father and the flight of the son, he cries:

> Then comes my fit again. I had else been perfect,
> Whole as the marble, founded as the rock,
> As broad and general as the casing air:
> But now I am cabin'd, cribb'd, confin'd, bound in
> To saucy doubts and fears.

It is mainly on this speech that those who hold absurd the idea that Macbeth was the Third Murderer rest their case, proof, they say, that the news of Fleance's escape came to him as a surprise. But others think the lines have the same marks of insincerity combined with unconscious truth as those in which Macbeth pretended to be surprised and horrified at the death of Duncan.

All this about the Third Murderer will be particularly abhorrent to "realists," who would bring everything to the bar of the senses, and logicians, whose fundamental axiom is that a thing cannot both be and not be at the same time. One wonders if they never had a dream in which one of the actors both was and was not a character from so-called "real" life. Anything that can happen in a dream can happen in poetry. Indeed this scene in which Banquo dies seems one of the most remarkable confirmations in Shakespeare of Nietzsche's main thesis in *The Birth of Tragedy,* that dreams and the drama come out of a common root. When an audience gathers in a theater, they come, if the play is worthy of the theater's great tradition, not to behold a transcript of the same old daylight life, but to dream together. In his bed a man dreaming is cut off from all social life. In the theater he is dreaming one dream with his fellows.

### VII

From his encounter with the ghost of Banquo at the banquet, Macbeth, too deep in blood to turn back, repairs at the beginning of act 4 to the Witches' cavern, bent on extorting the truth about the future, however bad, from these "filthy hags," as he calls them in self-torture. Which raises the question we have intentionally postponed: Who are the Weird Sisters? The Fates? Just three old women? Or something between the two?

Their own reference to "our masters" would rule out the idea that they are The Fates or The Norns, if nothing else did. Bradley declares without qualification: "There is not a syllable in *Macbeth* to imply that they are anything but women." But certainly almost every syllable of the play that has to do with them implies that, whatever they are, they are in intimate contact with that dark Underworld with the existence of which the play is centrally concerned. "In accordance with the popular ideas," Bradley goes on to say, "they have received from evil spirits certain supernatural powers," to control the weather, for example, to become invisible, to foresee the future, and so on. So when we behold them actually doing these things in the play it makes little difference whether we consider them supernatural beings themselves or women who have sold their souls to supernatural beings. The impression in either case is the same: that of demi-creatures, agents and procurers of those powers that, when men's wills falter, pull them down out of their freedom as the earth does the body of a bird whose wings have failed.

At the outset there is something mysterious and wonderful about the Witches, but they grow progressively more noisome and disgusting as Macbeth yields to them. Such is ever the relation of temptation to sin. The poet has shown us various earlier stages of moral disintegration in Henry IV, Henry V, Brutus, Hamlet, and others. Here is the same thing carried immeasurably further. It is as if man's integrity, once having begun to split up, tends to divide further and further, like the process of organic growth reversed. The Witches, representing this process, resemble fragments of those who, having taken and failed the human test, would revenge themselves on those who are trying to pass it by dragging them back to chaos. "They met me in the day of success!" It is easier to fall than to fly, to destroy than to create, to become like matter than to become like light. Whoever enlists on the side of destruction becomes in that sense an agent of fate.

The ingredients of the Witches' caldron confirm this conception of them. Those ingredients are things that in mythology and superstition, in the old natural philosophy and in our own ancestral consciousness, are associated with the darkest and cruelest elements of human nature: things voracious like the shark, sinister like the bat, poisonous like the adder, or ravenous like the wolf—and of these only fragments, preferably their most noxious or loathsome parts, the tooth, the scale, the sting, the maw, the gall, the entrails. To this predominantly animal brew are added a few vegetable elements, like hemlock and yew, suggestive of death and the grave, and a few reputedly subhuman ones from Turk or Tartar. A baboon's blood cools the whole.

Here Shakespeare is merely reiterating in intensified symbolic form what he has said from the beginning about unregulated appetite and passion. Here, recompounded into a sort of infernal quintessence, is the worst in the spirits of such men as Cardinal Pandulph and Cardinal Beaufort, of Don John and John of Lancaster, of Thersites and Iago. It is as if human nature, which never developed a special gland for the secretion of venom, tends when it degenerates to turn every organ—hand, lip, and brain—into such a gland. The whole body exudes malice and spite of life. The witches are embodiments of this death-force. Women? Of course—and who has not seen and turned away in horror from just this malevolence in some shrunken old crone? And yet not women—under-women who have regressed beyond the distinctions of sex.

> You should be women,
> And yet your beards forbid me to interpret
> That you are so.

How fitting, after man has done his utmost through war to bring disorder, that the cause of still further dissipation toward chaos should pass, when war closes, into the hands of these wizened hags, the natural representatives of the metaphysically female role of matter in the universe! Earth we think of as clean and beautiful, but spirit gone back to matter is, in all senses, another matter. It is then something miasmic and rotten. "Lilies that fester smell far worse than weeds." It is not just the battlefield covered with things torn and mangled. It is the battlefield after the stench and the putrefaction have set in. The witches in *Macbeth* are perhaps the completest antitypes to peace in Shakespeare.

The play presents explicitly the relation of Macbeth to the witches. It leaves implicit Lady Macbeth's relation to them, which is all the more interesting on that account. They do not need to accost her on any blasted heath. She herself invites them into her heart.

> Hie thee hither,

she cries to her husband when she has read his letter,

> That I may pour my spirits in thine ear.

But who are her spirits? We do not have to wait long to know. A messenger enters with word that "the King comes here to-night." Whereupon Lady Macbeth, in a passage that is the very prophecy and counterpart of the caldron scene, summons her spirits, the murdering ministers that wait on nature's mischief—a very definition of the Weird Sisters—calling on them to unsex her, to cram her with cruelty from top to toe, to turn her milk to gall. That ought to be enough. But Shakespeare makes the connection even more concrete. In planning the murder of Duncan, it is Lady Macbeth who, Circe-like, suggests that Duncan's chamberlains be transformed to beasts by wine and the guilt for the King's death laid at their door:

> When in *swinish* sleep
> Their drenched natures lie as in a death,
> What cannot you and I perform upon
> The unguarded Duncan?
>
> [author's italics]

It is this cowardly stratagem which finally convinces Macbeth that the enterprise is safe, and which leads, when the murder is discovered, to the unpremeditated death of the chamberlains at Macbeth's hands.

> FIRST WITCH: Where hast thou been, sister?
> SECOND WITCH: Killing *swine.*
>
> [author's italics]

The second witch and Lady Macbeth are about the same business. Who can question who poured the suggestion into Lady Macbeth's ear, and helped Macbeth to execute it later? It is the Adam and Eve story over again, with the witches in the role of the Serpent. Yet these same witches are powerless over those who do not meet them halfway:

> THIRD WITCH: Sister, where thou?
> FIRST WITCH: A sailor's wife had chestnuts in her lap,
> And munch'd, and munch'd, and munch'd.
> "Give me," quoth I.
> "Aroint thee, witch!" the rump-fed ronyon cries.

The witch is impotent under the exorcism, and swears to try her luck in revenge on the woman's sailor husband. So little, Shakespeare thus makes plain, is there any fatalism involved in the proximity of the Weird Sisters where a resolute will resists. Fire is hot. And fire is fascinating to a child. If the child goes too near the fire, he will be burned. We may call it fate if we will. It is in that conditional sense only that there is any fatalism in *Macbeth*.

## VIII

The end of the story is mainly an account of how these two once human beings pass into that subhuman realm of disintegration where the witches are at home. One is pushed into the abyss as it were by her memories. The other leaps into it fanatically, as if embracing it. Her fall is primarily pitiful; his, fearful.

Because, before the deed, Lady Macbeth suffered from defect of imagination and excess of propensity to act, her punishment, in compensation, takes the form of being pursued, as by furies, by her memories, by the facts of the past. "How easy is it, then!" she had said. "What's done cannot be undone," she says now. Formerly she scorned her husband for his moments of abstraction:

> Be not lost
> So poorly in your thoughts.

Now she is not only lost but buried in her own, abstracted to the point of somnambulism.

> Come, thick night,
> And pall thee in the dunnest smoke of hell,

she had prayed on the verge of the first murder. "Hell is murky!" she mutters in the sleepwalking scene. Her prayer is answered. She is there. She has a light with her continually in a vain attempt to shut out the images that follow one another in perpetual succession. The blood runs from the old man's body unendingly. She washes her hands over and over. Such a circle is madness. Lady Macbeth is caught in it. She prefers death.

Because Macbeth saw the horror in advance and shrank from action, yet let himself be enticed on into it, only to wish his crime undone the moment he had committed it, his punishment takes the form of a fury of deeds. He meets anywhere, in full daylight, the specters that at first came to him only by twilight or at night. If hers is a retrospective and nocturnal, his is a diurnal and dramatic nightmare. If she is transported to an underworld, he transforms his own life into hell. It becomes an alternation of fear and fury. His perpetual reassurance to himself that he cannot know fear is a measure of the fear he feels. As his hand once dyed the world red, his heart now paints it a sickly white. "Cream-fac'd loon! . . . lily-liver'd boy . . . linen cheeks . . . wheyface." These are not so much descriptions of what he sees as projections of what he feels. "Hang those that talk of fear" might be his command for his own death. Now he would have his armor put on, now pulled off. The two moods follow each other with lightninglike rapidity.

> I pull in resolution.
>   . . . Arm, arm, and out! . . .
> I 'gin to be aweary of the sun,
>   . . . Blow, wind! come, wrack!
> At least we'll die with harness on our back.

These oscillations in less than a dozen lines. And between the fear and the fury, moments of blank apathy culminating, when Lady Macbeth's death is announced, in the famous

> To-morrow, and to-morrow, and to-morrow,

the *ne plus ultra* in English words of the meaninglessness of life—

>                a tale
> Told by an idiot, full of sound and fury,
> Signifying nothing.

This is Hamlet's sterile promontory, his foul and pestilent congregation of vapors, his quintessence of dust, carried to their nadir. The kingdom Macbeth's ambition has conquered turns out to be a limbo of blank idiocy.

Of Macbeth's physical bravery at the end too much has been made, for it is mainly desperation. There are other things that help him retain our sympathy more than that.

> They have tied me to a stake; I cannot fly,
> But, bear-like, I must fight the course.

That might well be the memory of some bearbaiting Shakespeare witnessed as a boy. And another touch pierces even deeper. When Macduff finally confronts the object of his revenge, crying, "Turn, hell-hound, turn!" Macbeth exclaims:

> Of all men else I have avoided thee.
> But get thee back; my soul is too much charg'd
> With blood of thine already.

It is his sole confession of remorse. But like one star in the blackness it is the brighter on that account.


## IX

The fourth act of *Macbeth* has been accused of sagging. It has even been pronounced "tedious." After the concentration of the first three acts on the two central characters, a fourth act which omits both of them except for its first scene is bound to fall off somewhat in interest. Yet the long passage in which Malcolm tests Macduff, to make certain that he is not a hidden agent of Macbeth, is just one more variation of the mousetrap situation in *Hamlet,* with echoes of the casket theme from *The Merchant of Venice* and a touch, in reverse, of the temptation scene from *Othello*. If a passage with such patterns behind it is found wanting in dramatic tension, it is surely more the actors' or reader's fault than Shakespeare's. In it Malcolm reveals on a smaller scale some of the most engaging traits of Hamlet: something of the same modesty, wisdom, circumspection, and poetic insight, the same tendency to dramatize himself, to pass himself off for less than he is, to lie low and play psychological games on others, but without a trace of Hamlet's antic disposition. He speaks in this scene mainly about evil, but in doing so his vocabulary manages to be full of such words as angels, grace, child, snow, lamb, milk. If we know Shakespeare, we know what this means. The man's imagination is contradicting his intellect. His metaphors are giving away the deeper truth. He speaks of himself as "a weak poor innocent lamb," yet proceeds a few lines later to assert that he is so full of

> All the particulars of vice so grafted,
> That, when they shall be open'd, black Macbeth
> Will seem as pure as snow, and the poor state
> Esteem him as a lamb, being compar'd
> With my confineless harms.

The projection on Macbeth of the attributes of snow and of the lamb need not deceive us as to whose they really are.

> Nay, had I power, I should
> Pour the sweet milk of concord into hell.

This is a sort of inverted or celestial irony. Malcolm thinks he is stigmatizing himself as the undying enemy of peace, but over his head the words are a prophecy that, when he comes to the throne, his love of peace will assuage the infernal state to which Scotland has been reduced under Macbeth. At the sight of Macduff's genuine grief Malcolm is convinced of his integrity and abjures the "taints and blames" he has just laid on himself as bait. In his retraction, however, he does not claim for himself "the king-becoming graces" he previously listed as his deficiencies, but we more than suspect that he possesses something of every one of them. The mere fact that he is able to give us the most nearly perfect picture in Shakespeare of the ideal king is in itself significant. He seems to have inherited the gentleness of his father along with a greater valor. The outlook for Scotland under him is bright.

## X

At the end of the interview between Malcolm and Macduff comes the passage describing the heavenly gifts and graces of the English king (Edward the Confessor), particularly his power to cure "the evil" by royal touch. Historical scholarship tells us that here Shakespeare turns aside from his play to pay a compliment to King James. Doubtless he does pay such a compliment. But that he turns aside to do it is not so certain. Here, to begin with, is the most effective of contrasts between the English king and the Scottish tyrant. More than that. Here is explicitly announced the contra-theme to the main subject of the play. That subject is human traffic with infernal spirits. But King Edward—though "how he solicits heaven, Himself best knows"—has the capacity to become the agent of celestial powers, can use spiritual force to heal rather than to destroy, is an instrument not of darkness but of light. Nothing could be less of a digression than this passage. Without it, and without various little touches throughout the play that support what it says, the play would be a different thing. It is one thing to believe in infernal spirits alone, quite another to believe in both infernal and celestial ones.

Our age speaks of its own spiritual unrest, thinks it permissible to believe in spiritual influences and tendencies, but holds it rank superstition to believe in spirits. It wants the adjective without the noun. The absurdity of this position was long ago demonstrated once for all by Socrates in the *Apology:*

> Did ever man, Meletus, believe in the existence of human things, and not human beings? . . . Did ever any man believe in horsemanship, and not in horses? or in flute-playing, and not in flute-players? No, my friend; I will answer to you and to the court, as you refuse to answer for yourself. There is no man who ever did. But now please to answer the next question: *Can a man believe in spiritual and divine agencies, and not in spirits or demigods?*

And Meletus, driven to the wall, admits, "He can not."

Where there is a gravitational pull, there must be a mass of matter pulling. Where there is illumination, there must be something emitting light. Where there is attribute, there must be substance. Over thousands of years the habits of the human imagination in this matter have never deviated. Socrates and Shakespeare are obedient to them. Those habits, we may be certain, have not been altered by the materialisms and rationalisms of a few generations of the nineteenth and twentieth centuries. During those generations it became fashionable to believe that things psychical are a sort of product or secretion of the brain. Faced suddenly with psychic reality itself, as it has been in two world wars, this unheroic philosophy now cries out in consternation with Macbeth:

> The time has been,
> That, when the brains were out, the man would die,
> And there an end; but now they rise again
> With twenty mortal murders on their crowns
> And push us from our stools. This is more strange
> Than such a murder is.

It is indeed, and from end to end the play is saturated with this strangeness. We put it down with the ineradicable conviction that the instruments of darkness of which it tells are real. It has exposed the sensitive imagination to an experience which otherwise only personal indulgence in cruelty might impart.

There are some human consciousnesses, says John Cowper Powys, who are tempted to give themselves up to a pleasure in cruelty; but if they knew the unspeakable ghastliness of the reality they are thus creating for themselves, they would stop dead, *there* where they stand, with a shiver of para- lyzed self-loathing. That such cruelty is suicidal from a hu- man stand-point, they know well. They know the ordi- nary human hell they are preparing for themselves. What they don't seem to know is the far worse cosmic Terror they are bringing down upon them. Insanity, that's what it is; not merely human insanity, but unutterable, unspeak- able, *nonhuman insanity.* Sometimes in dreams of the night people who have been deliberately cruel get a glimpse of what they have done, and *what companions they have now got.*

The psychology of cruelty is a strange thing. The cruel person says to himself: "I have got beyond human law and human feeling. All is now permitted me, if I can but harden my heart." Little does he know! Better had he never been born *than have gone where he has gone* and at- tached to himself the ghastliness of the abyss that now clings to him. The "Hell" of the mediaeval imagination is a poetical joke compared with what he is on the way to experience—crying indeed "upon the mountains to cover him and the floods to overwhelm him"! Horror is a very peculiar and a very appalling thing; and those who have peeped through the cosmic chink into the Horror-Dance of the abyss would sooner henceforth hold their hands in a candle-flame and burn them to the bone, than give them- selves up to deliberate cruelty.

This is precisely the Horror encountered at death by Kurtz, the Eu- ropean who reverted to African savagery, in Conrad's *Heart of Dark- ness.* It is the Horror of which Henry James gives more than a glimpse in *The Turn of the Screw.*

## XI

But now at the end comes the strangest and most paradoxical fact about this play. And the loveliest. If *Macbeth* is Shakespeare's Descent into Hell, it is also his spring myth. This picture of blackness is framed in light, placed, we might almost say, against a background of verdure.

Shakespeare announces this theme, however faintly, in the first pages of the play. The bleeding Sergeant brings word that peace has been made with the rebels but that fresh war at the same moment has broken out with Norway. So storms, he says, sometimes come from the east where the sun rises, or discomfort from spring which promises comfort. Since word is immediately brought that Macbeth has averted the new threat with a second victory, we dismiss the Sergeant's metaphor from mind, not noticing how much better it fits the play as a whole than the minor incidents to which he applies it. For what is the tyranny of Macbeth between the reigns of Duncan and Malcolm but winter come back after the promise of spring only to be overcome in turn by spring itself? For, however delayed, spring always wins. So Malcolm and Macduff subdue the tyrant and Scotland looks forward to a dispensation of peace. Thus does a figure from its first page impart to the play its underlying pattern.

All this, however well it fits, might seem like making too much out of a metaphor thrown out so casually, if we did not know Shakespeare's habit of announcing important themes in the opening lines of his plays, and if, in this case, he had not so strikingly confirmed at the end what he hints at in the beginning. I refer to the coming of Birnam Wood to Dunsinane. When each of Malcolm's soldiers hews down a branch and bears it before him, it is only in a manner of speaking that the forest moves. But it does move in another and lovelier sense. The legend Shakespeare makes use of is a myth of the coming of spring. "The legend of the moving forest originated in the German religious custom of May-festivals, or summer welcomings, and . . . King Grunenwald is originally a winter giant whose dominion ceases when the May feast begins and the greenwood draws near."

War is winter. Peace is spring. Were ever symbols more inevitable than these, especially in the religion and poetry of northern peoples? Winter is a giant. Spring, in comparison, is a maiden. How powerless she seems in his presence! But because the sun is on her side and moves in every root and bud she undermines the sway of the tyrant. She has great allies. And so does peace in this play. The Old Man, for instance, who talks with Ross outside the castle and bids him farewell in those Desdemona-like words:

> God's benison go with you; and with those
> That would make good of bad, and friends of foes;

the Doctor who says at the sight of Lady Macbeth,

> More needs she the divine than the physician.
> God, God forgive us all!

the Waiting-Gentlewoman who bids him, "Good-night, good doctor"; little Macduff; the pious King Edward. These, and others, play no conspicuous part in the story. Yet perhaps Shakespeare is implying that it is only by the collaboration of thousands like them, whose contributions singly may seem as insignificant as single grassblades do to spring, that war, like winter, can be overcome.

# *Macbeth*: A Lust for Power

## *L. C. Knights*

Macbeth defines a particular kind of evil—the evil that results from a lust for power. The defining, as in all the tragedies, is in strictly poetic and dramatic terms. It is certainly not an abstract formulation, but lies rather in the drawing out of necessary consequences and implications of that lust both in the external and the spiritual worlds. Its meaning, therefore, is revealed in the expansion and unfolding of what lies within the initial evil, in terms of direct human experience. The logic is not formal but experiential, and demands from us, if we are to test its validity and feel its force, a fulness of imaginative response and a closeness of realization, in which both sensation and feeling become modes of understanding. Only when intellect, emotion, and a kind of direct sensory awareness work together can we enter fully into that exploratory and defining process.

In other words, the essential structure of *Macbeth,* as of the other tragedies, is to be sought in the poetry. That of course is easily said; what it means is something that can only be grasped in relation to specific instances or not grasped at all. We may take as an example Macbeth's "aside" when he has been greeted as Thane of Cawdor.

> This supernatural soliciting
> Cannot be ill; cannot be good:—
> If ill, why hath it given me earnest of success,
> Commencing in a truth? I am Thane of Cawdor:

From *Some Shakespearean Themes.* © 1959 by L. C. Knights. Stanford University Press, 1959.

> If good, why do I yield to that suggestion
> Whose horrid image doth unfix my hair,
> And make my seated heart knock at my ribs,
> Against the use of nature? Present fears
> Are less than horrible imaginings.
> My thought, whose murder yet is but fantastical,
> Shakes so my single state of man,
> That function is smother'd in surmise,
> And nothing is, but what is not.
>
> (1.3.130–42)

This is temptation, presented with concrete force. Even if we attend only to the revelation of Macbeth's spiritual state, our recognition of the body—the very feel—of the experience, is a response to the poetry, to such things as the sickening seesaw rhythm ("Cannot be ill; cannot be good") changing to the rhythm of the pounding heart, the overriding of grammar ("My thought, whose murder yet is but fantastical") as thought is revealed in the very process of formation, and so on. But the poetry makes further claims, and if we attend to them we find that the words do not only point inward to the presumed state of Macbeth's mind but, as it were, outward to the play as a whole. The equivocal nature of temptation, the commerce with phantoms consequent upon false choice, the resulting sense of unreality ("nothing is, but what is not"), which has yet such power to "smother" vital function, the unnaturalness of evil ("against the use of nature"), and the relation between disintegration in the individual ("my single state of man") and disorder in the larger social organism—all these are major themes of the play which are mirrored in the speech under consideration. They emerge as themes because they are what the poetry—reinforced by action and symbolism—again and again insists on. And the interrelations we are forced to make take us outside the speeches of the protagonist to the poetry of the play as a whole. That "smother'd," for example, takes us forward not only to Lady Macbeth's "blanket of the dark" but to such things as Ross's choric comment after the murder of Duncan:

> by th' clock 'tis day,
> And yet dark night strangles the travelling lamp.
> Is't night's predominance, or the day's shame,
> That darkness does the face of earth entomb,
> When living light should kiss it?
>
> (2.4.6–10)

In none of the tragedies is there anything superfluous, but it is perhaps *Macbeth* that gives the keenest impression of economy. The action moves directly and quickly to the crisis, and from the crisis to the full working out of plot and theme. The pattern is far easier to grasp than that of *Lear.* The main theme of the reversal of values is given out simply and clearly in the first scene—"Fair is foul, and foul is fair"; and with it are associated premonitions of the conflict, disorder and moral darkness into which Macbeth will plunge himself. Well before the end of the first act we are in possession not only of the positive values against which the Macbeth evil will be defined but of the related aspects of that evil, which is simultaneously felt as a strained and unnatural perversion of the will, an obfuscation of the clear light of reason, a principle of disorder (both in the "single state of man" and in his wider social relations), and a pursuit of illusions. All these impressions, which as the play proceeds assume the status of organizing ideas, are produced by the interaction of all the resources of poetic drama—action, contrast, statement, implication, imagery and allusion. Thus the sense of the unnaturalness of evil is evoked not only by repeated explicit references ("nature's mischief," "nature seems dead," "'Tis unnatural, even like the deed that's done," and so on) but by the expression of unnatural sentiments and an unnatural violence of tone in such things as Lady Macbeth's invocation of the "spirits" who will "unsex" her, and her affirmation that she would murder the babe at her breast if she had sworn to do it. So too the theme of the false appearances inseparable from evil, of deceit recoiling on the deceiver, is not only the subject of explicit comment

> —And be these juggling fiends no more believ'd,
> That palter with us in a double sense—
>
> (5.8.19–20)

it is embodied in the action, so that Macbeth's despairing recognition of mere "mouth-honour" among his remaining followers (5.3.27) echoes ironically his wife's advice to "look like th' innocent flower, But be the serpent under't" (1.5.64–65) and the hypocritical play of the welcoming of Duncan; and it is reinforced by—or indeed one with—the evoked sense of equivocation and evasiveness associated with the witches, and the cloud of uncertainty that settles on Scotland during Macbeth's despotism. It is fitting that the final movement of the reversal that takes place in the last act should open with the command of Malcolm to the camouflaged soldiers, "Your leavy screens throw down, And show like those you are" (5.6.1–2).

## II

The assurance of *Macbeth* has behind it, is indeed based on, a deeply imagined resolution of perplexities inherent in any full exposure to life. Freedom from the tyranny of time and illusion is finally related, at the deepest levels of consciousness, to the central affirmations of the spirit; and conversely, the obsessed awareness of time without meaning, like the subjection of mind to appearance, is revealed not simply as consequential on false choice but as intrinsic to it: for "the eye altering alters all." There is a similar assurance in the use of "nature," in that aspect of the play's imaginative structure that impels us to say not merely that Macbeth's crime is unnatural (*i.e.,* inhuman) but that the values against which evil is defined are in some sense grounded in nature. To suggest how this is so, to relate the insights operative here to those already touched on, it is necessary to step back from the play and to see it in the wider context of Shakespeare's development as a whole. Although in recent years much has been written about the meanings of nature in Shakespeare and his contemporaries, there is still need for further clarification of the perceptions controlling the use of this elusive, indispensable and pregnant word.

In Shakespeare's poetic thought we find two apparently contradictory intuitions regarding man's relation to the created world existing independently of human choice and will. Nature and human values are felt as intimately related, and at the same time as antagonistic.

They are related in two ways. Shakespeare, like almost all poets, uses natural imagery to evoke and define qualities that are humanly valuable, indeed indispensable to any full humanity:

> She that herself will sliver and disbranch
> From her material sap, perforce must wither
> And come to deadly use.

> For his bounty,
> There was no winter in't; an autumn 'twas
> That grew the more by reaping.

These are striking instances, but in even apparently casual metaphors and similes—"my love is all as boundless as the sea," "and she in thee Calls back the lovely April of her prime," "as dear to me as are the ruddy drops that visit my sad heart"—it seems that we have to do with a relationship more intimate than that of mere resemblance: the mind has in some sense *found itself* in nature; for, as Leone Vivante says of Shakespeare's images of budding and of morning, "the grace of things in their birth and their first purity would not be perceived, if it were not *first* a quality of our mental synthesis which is revealed in and through them." This is indeed a truth of general application; Blake's Tiger, Herbert's Flower, Marvell's Garden (in the poems of those names), and Wordsworth's

> uncertain heaven, received
> Into the bosom of the steady lake,
> (*The Prelude*, 5.387–88)

all imply a basic kinship of human and nonhuman life: mind would be less truly itself if it were not deeply responsive to images such as these. The correspondences between mind and natural forms and natural processes is attested by common speech as well as by the poets. Just as it is with peculiar rightness that George Herbert can say, "And now in age I bud again," or that Marvell can speak of "a green thought in a green shade," so images of budding, growing, harvesting, of night, dawn and day, of seasons and weathers, of climates and landscapes, are integral to the speech in which we ourselves feel after inner experience.

> *La Nature est un temple où de vivants piliers*
> *Laissent parfois sortir de confuses paroles;*
> *L'homme y passe à travers des forêts de symboles*
> *Qui l'observent avec des regards familiers.*

In Shakespeare there is no attempt to explain the working of these *regards familiers;* but the mere fact that his plays and poems are full of these more-than-analogies implies that psychic life is at home in nature.

But even if we leave aside the difficult question of natural symbolism, there is no doubt that wherever Shakespeare envisages a fully human way of life he thinks of it as closely related to the wider setting of organic growth, as indeed, in a quite concrete and practical way, directly based on man's dealings with the earth that nourishes him. It is of course in *The Winter's Tale* that we are most explicitly aware of nature as a powerful controlling presence—a presence moreover not vaguely felt but specifically rendered in the great pastoral scene with its many reminders of seasonal activities, humble in themselves but translucent to the great myths. But Shakespeare's vision of the intimate relationship between man and nature, of nature as the necessary basis and, under certain conditions, the pattern for civilization, goes back to the period before the final plays and before the tragedies. It is expressed in the beautiful but strangely neglected speech of Burgundy, in *King Henry V,* when he urges peace.

> let it not disgrace me
> If I demand before this royal view,
> Why that the naked, poor, and mangled Peace,
> Dear nurse of arts, plenties, and joyful births,
> Should not in this best garden of the world,
> Our fertile France, put up her lovely visage?
> Alas! she hath from France too long been chas'd,
> And all her husbandry doth lie on heaps,
> Corrupting in its own fertility.
> Her vine, the merry cheerer of the heart,
> Unpruned dies; her hedges even-pleach'd
> Like prisoners wildly overgrown with hair,
> Put forth disorder'd twigs; her fallow leas
> The darnel, hemlock and rank fumitory
> Doth root upon, while that the coulter rusts
> That should deracinate such savagery;
> The even mead, that erst brought sweetly forth
> The freckled cowslip, burnet, and green clover,
> Wanting the scythe, all uncorrected, rank,
> Conceives by idleness, and nothing teems
> But hateful docks, rough thistles, kecksies, burrs,
> Losing both beauty and utility.
> And as our vineyards, fallows, meads, and hedges,
> Defective in their natures, grow to wildness,
> Even so our houses and ourselves and children
> Have lost, or do not learn for want of time,
> The sciences that should become our country,
> But grow like savages, as soldiers will
> That nothing do but meditate on blood,

> To swearing and stern looks, defus'd attire,
> And every thing that seems unnatural.
>
> (5.2.31–62)

There is here an imaginative vision that transcends the simple sequence of the argument. After the preliminary invocation of peace the passage is built on a simple inversion: uncultivated nature ("corrupting in its own fertility"—a phrase that Milton must have remembered) is compared to disorderly or uncultivated human life, which in turn is compared to "wild" or "savage" nature. But what we have to deal with is something more complex than a simple comparison which is then given again with the terms reversed; Burgundy is throughout expressing a sense of the interrelationship—a two-way traffic—between man and nature. Natural fertility ("our fertile France") is the necessary precondition not only of life at the biological level but of the highest reaches of manmade civilization—the "arts" and "sciences" (both of which can be interpreted in the widest sense); whilst at the same time, since peace is the nurse not only of these but of all that comes to birth, of the very fertility on which the whole range of human activity depends, and since it is man who *makes* peace, man is responsible for nature. The alternative to peace is "wildness" in both man and nature, and for man to tame that wildness in himself is a process analogous to taming what is given in external nature. So much is stated or directly suggested: what is not quite explicit but imaginatively present, adding life and vibrancy to the flat prose-meaning to which I have reduced the poetry, is the vision of peace. Conceived throughout as a wholesome *activity*— "laying" hedges, ploughing, and so on are taken as representative examples—it is a state in which arts and sciences and daily beauty and utility are conceived both as end and as condition of the fertility on which all alike depend. Behind the image of life and nature run wild for lack of human care is the implied ideal of natural force tended and integrated into a truly human civilization. And the inclusive "Peace," teeming with human activity, is the "natural" end of the "joyful births": it is the alternative "wildness" that is "unnatural."

But if Burgundy's speech, looking forward as it does to *The Winter's Tale,* represents an important element in Shakespeare's imaginative vision of man and nature, there is also another, its polar opposite, of which a brief reminder will serve. If nature is bounty she is also decay; she is the ally of chance in "untrimming" "every fair" (Sonnet 18); it is the same sky that indifferently "cheers" and "checks" both men and flowers (Sonnet 15). Worse still, if nature as the world of organic growth and decay is indifferent to human needs, as instinct and appetite ("blood") she can be positively hostile to the life of the spirit. And between "natural law" as traditionally understood (i.e., reason) and the law of nature by which, as Falstaff lightly remarked, the young dace is a bait for the old pike, there is an absolute distinction.

All this Shakespeare knew well enough, and in *King Lear,* addressing himself to the question of man's place in nature, and with a full view of all the potential evil in man as part of nature, he magnificently reaffirmed the autonomy of the spirit. Yet in Shakespeare's poetic thought the idea of relationship to nature seems as integral as the idea of the fundamental difference between the two realms. The question we are forced to ask, therefore, is, If human nature is not entirely at home in the world of nature, if in some essential ways it is set over against nature, how can mind find itself in nature, as there is such abundant testimony that it does? How is it that in *Macbeth* (to be specific) essential distinctions of good and evil, belonging to the inner world, can be defined in imagery of the outer world of nature, defined moreover in such a way that the imaginative correspondence goes far beyond the use of selected analogies and implies a symbolic equivalence—indeed a relationship—between what is "natural" for man and what is "natural" in the simplest and widest sense of the word?

We are led back once more to *King Lear,* to one scene in particular where we first become conscious of a change in direction of the imaginative current of the play, as though a slight but unmistakable breeze were announcing that a tide, still at the ebb, is about to turn. In the opening scenes of act 4 the worst is still to come; both Gloucester and Lear have still to reach the lowest point of their despair. But Gloucester, we know, is in the care of Edgar, and in the fourth scene, immediately after we have been told of Lear's purgatorial shame, Cordelia enters, "with drum and colours," seeking her father.

> CORDELIA: Alack! 'tis he: why, he was met even now
> As mad as the vex'd sea; singing aloud;
> Crown'd with rank fumiter and furrow-weeds,
> With hardocks, hemlock, nettles, cuckoo-flowers,
> Darnel, and all the idle weeds that grow

In our sustaining corn. A century sent forth;
Search every acre in the high-grown field,
And bring him to our eye. [*Exit* AN OFFICER.]
                    What can man's wisdom
In the restoring his bereaved sense?
He that helps him take all my outward worth.

DOCTOR: There is means, madam;
Our foster-nurse of nature is repose,
The which he lacks; that to provoke in him,
Are many simples operative, whose power
Will close the eye of anguish.

CORDELIA:          All bless'd secrets,
All you unpublish'd virtues of the earth,
Spring with my tears! be aidant and remediate
In the good man's distress! Seek, seek for him,
Lest his ungovern'd rage dissolve the life
That wants the means to lead it.

                            (4.4.1–20)

What is remarkable here is the particular quality of the awareness of nature that lies behind and informs the poetry. Lear's "ungovern'd rage" is compared, as before, to elemental fury ("as mad as the vex'd sea"), and his mock crown is fittingly made up of "idle weeds," astonishingly present in the clogged movement of the lines that list them. Yet co-present with these—and given emphasis by the lift and smooth sweep of the verse—is "our sustaining corn"; and the same earth bears the medicinal plants that foster restoring sleep ("balm of hurt minds, great nature's second course"). Nature, then, is contemplated in both its aspects, as that which preserves and as that which impedes, encroaches on or rises in turmoil against man's specifically human activities; and it is contemplated with a peculiar serenity. It is of course contemplated from the standpoint of Cordelia; and her qualities—those particularly that lie behind this serenity—have been explicitly and beautifully evoked in the immediately preceding scene. The law of her nature, it is clear, is quite other than the law of nature to which Goneril and Regan abandon themselves:—

                it seem'd she was a queen
Over her passion; who, most rebel-like,
Sought to be king o'er her.

                            (4.3.14–16)

Yet there is nothing rigid in this self-control. She is mov'd, though "not to a rage"; and we feel it fitting that one so far removed from all that is merely natural should yet attract to herself images and associations from the world of nature,

> patience and sorrow strove
> Who should express her goodliest. You have seen
> Sunshine and rain at once; her smiles and tears
> Were like, a better way,
>
> (4.3.18–20)

just as it is perfectly in keeping that religious associations—"There she shook the holy water from her heavenly eyes" (4.3.30–31)— should almost immediately blend with those of "sunshine and rain at once". What we are given in the poetry is a sure and sensitive poise, and it is Cordelia's integrity—her tenderness, as we have seen, at one with her strength—that explains her full and ready responsiveness. It is because she is fully human—though there are also potent suggestions of divine grace—that she is "natural" in a different sense from that intended in Edmund's philosophy. Her sense of the bounty of nature (of "our sustaining corn" as well as of the "rank fumiter and furrow-weeds") lies behind her invocation,—

> All bless'd secrets,
> All you unpublish'd virtues of the earth,
> Spring with my tears! be aidant and remediate
> In the good man's distress!

But it is because of her love and pity ("the good man" is the erring Lear) that she can invoke so whole-heartedly the "unpublish'd virtues of the earth"—can invoke them moreover not simply as allies from a different realm, but with a suggestion of kinship and intimacy that almost equates their working with the power of outgoing and healing life that lies deep in the soul. It is in this sense that Cordelia "redeems nature from the general curse Which twain have brought her to" (4.4.207–8).

It is this complex resolution of feeling, issuing in new insight, that lies behind the use of "nature" in *Macbeth*. Since the insight stems from a mode of being and is inseparable from it, it cannot be summed up in a formula. But in matters of this kind simple formulations have their uses, if only as a way of ensuring that necessary complexity has not, in the course of argument, degenerated into mere verbal complication, or that mountains are not being made out of molehills. Shakespeare, then, does not say that "nature, however inscrutable, is basically beneficent"; he does not say that there is "in nature a core of tenderness, which lies even deeper than pride or cruelty". He says—though it takes the whole of *King Lear* to say it adequately—that nature *per se* is something quite other than human nature, and that it cannot properly be conceived in human terms; that its humanly relevant quality only exists in relation to a particular human outlook and standpoint; and that what that quality is depends on the standpoint from which the relation is established. "Nature-as-beneficent" is a concept that only has meaning for the good man—or at all events for the man who admits the imperatives of his own humanity. Perhaps it is easier to grasp this in relation to the world—the given "nature"—of inner experience. The mind ("that ocean, where each kind does straight its own resemblance find") contains within itself elements corresponding to nonhuman life—Blake's tiger and lamb. So long as these natural forces are not integrated by the specifically human principle they are, or are likely to become, chaotic and destructive. Given that principle, they may be sublimated and transformed, but they are not disowned: they are freely accepted as the natural sources of life and power. So too with the external world of nature: it is only the man who recognizes his own humanity, and that of others, as something essentially other than a product of the natural world, who is really open to nature; neither fascinated nor afraid, he can respond creatively to its creativeness, and, paradoxically, find in nature a symbol for all that is natural in the other sense—that is, most truly human. It is, I think, some such perception as this, attained in *King Lear,* that lies behind and validates the elaborate and imaginatively powerful analogy between the human order and the order of nature in *Macbeth*.

### III

There is no vague "philosophy of nature" in *Macbeth*. The nature against which the "unnaturalness" of the Macbeth evil is defined and judged is human nature; and essential characteristics of that nature—its capacity for and intimate dependence on relationship—are powerfully evoked throughout the play. In act 3, scene 4 Macbeth, overcome by his vision of Banquo's ghost, glances back to a time when murder was common, to what will later be known as the Hobbesian state of nature.

> Blood hath been shed ere now, i' th' olden time,
> Ere humane statute purg'd the gentle weal;
> Ay, and since too, murthers have been perform'd
> Too terrible for the ear: the time has been,
> That, when the brains were out, the man would die,
> And there an end; but now, they rise again,
> With twenty mortal murthers on their crowns,
> And push us from our stools. This is more strange
> Than such a murther is.
>
> (3.4.74–82)

This is a more profound version of the origins of society than is suggested by the notion of contract or expediency. What "purges" the supposed mere multitude and makes it into a "gentle" common-weal is a decree greater than any law in which it may be embodied, for it is what is dictated by the very fact of being human; if you accept your humanity then you can't murder with impunity. Nor is this simply a matter of judicial punishment: the murdered man "rises" again, in you. Killing may be common in wild nature, but it is not natural to man as man; it is a violation of his essential humanity. When Lady Macbeth describes her husband as "too full o' the milk of human kindness" she intends to be disparaging, as Goneril does when she speaks of Albany's "milky gentleness" or calls him a "milk-liver'd man" (King Lear, 1.4.351; 4.2.50). But what the phrase also says is that human kindness is natural to man as man, and, like his mother's milk, nourishes his manhood. When Malcolm accuses himself of imaginary crimes, and in so doing reflects the evil that Macbeth has brought on Scotland, the climax is,

> Nay, had I power, I should
> Pour the sweet milk of concord into Hell,
> Uproar the universal peace, confound
> All unity in earth.
>
> (4.3.97–100)

"Concord," "peace," "unity"—these are *active* words, signifying not a mere absence of disagreeables, a mere deliverance from "continual fear, and danger of violent death," but the condition of positive human living. We learn little about a play by making lists of words, but it is a significant fact that *Macbeth* contains a very large number of words expressing the varied relations of life (not only "cousin," "children," "servants," "guest," "host," but "thanks," "payment," "service," "loyalty," "duties"), and that these sometimes, as in act 1 scenes 4 and 6, seem to be dwelt on with a special insistence. At the end of the play, when Macbeth thinks of what he has lost, it is not "honour, wealth and ease in waning age" (*Lucrece,* l. 142) but

> that which should accompany old age,
> As honour, love, obedience, troops of friends,
>
> (5.3.24–25)

An awareness of those "holy cords" which, though they may be severed, are "too intrince"—too intimately intertwined—"to un-loose" (*King Lear,* 2.2.75–76), is integral to the imaginative structure of *Macbeth.* That the man who breaks the bonds that tie him to other men, who "pours the sweet milk of concord into Hell," is at the same time violating his own nature and thwarting his own deepest needs, is something that the play dwells on with a special insistence.

Now as we have seen in relation to *King Lear* it is only when the essential needs and characteristics of human nature are given an absolute, unconditional priority, that nature in its widest sense can be invoked as an order underlying, invigorating, and in a certain sense offering a pattern for, human nature. So too in *Macbeth.* In Macbeth's apocalyptic soliloquy before the murder, the "Pity" that dominates the chaotic natural forces and rides the whirlwind appears as a new-born babe—an offspring of humanity, naked, vulnerable, and powerful. It is, we may say, because of the symbol of the babe, and all it stands for, that Shakespeare can invoke the powers of nature and associate them, as Professor Wilson Knight shows that he does, with all that is opposed to, and finally victorious over, the powers of destruction.

It is in the scene of Duncan's entry into Macbeth's castle (1.6.)— "a perfect contrast in microcosm to the Macbeth evil"—that we are most vividly aware of the energies of untaught nature in significant relation to the human order. The scene is set for full dramatic effect between Lady Macbeth's invocation of the powers of darkness ("The raven himself is hoarse, that croaks the fatal entrance") and Macbeth's final resolution, and Duncan's courtesy underlines the irony. But the contrast is not confined to the situation. The suggestion of a sweet fresh air, the pleased contemplation of the birds that build and breed, affect us first as sensory contrasts to the smothering oppression ("Come, thick Night") so recently evoked; but like the images of darkness and disorder the presented scene is inseparable from the values it embodies and defines.

> This guest of summer,
> The temple-haunting martlet, does approve,
> By his lov'd mansionry, that the heaven's breath
> Smells wooingly here: no jutty, frieze,
> Buttress, nor coign of vantage, but this bird
> Hath made his pendent bed, and procreant cradle:
> Where they most breed and haunt, I have observ'd
> The air is delicate.

What we are contemplating here is a natural and wholesome *order*, of which the equivalent in the human sphere is to be found in those mutualities of loyalty, trust and liking that Macbeth proposes to violate. And it is an order that is at one with the life it fosters. The opening lines of the scene, in short, are not only beautiful in themselves, they form an image of life delighting in life. It is in terms of destructive and self-destructive energies that Macbeth's power lust is defined; and it is from the "life" images of the play, which range from the temple-haunting martlets to Macduff's "babes," his "pretty ones," and include all the scattered references to man's natural goods—sleep and food and fellowship—that we take our bearings in the apprehension of evil.

## IV

In the great soliloquy of 1.7. Macbeth tries to provide himself with prudential reasons for not committing murder:—

> But in these cases,
> We still have judgment here; that we but teach
> Bloody instructions, which, being taught, return
> To plague th'inventor.

But the attempt at a cool calculation of consequences (already at odds with the nervous rhythm and the taut muscular force of the imagery of the opening lines) almost immediately gives way to an appalling vision of judgment.

> Besides, this Duncan
> Hath borne his faculties so meek, hath been
> So clear in his great office, that his virtues
> Will plead like angels, trumpet-tongu'd, against
> The deep damnation of his taking-off.

These lines have of course behind them the traditional conception of the Day of Judgment, and it is nothing less than the nature of judgment that the play reveals. Just as, in Spinoza's words "blessedness is not the reward of virtue but virtue itself," so the deep damnation of this play is revealed in the intrinsic qualities of an evil deliberately willed and persisted in. It is revealed above all as a defection from life and reality.

> So that in vent'ring ill we leave to be
> The things we are for that which we expect;
> And this ambitious foul infirmity,
> In having much, torments us with defect
> Of that we have: so then we do neglect
>     The things we have, and, all for want of wit,
>     Make something nothing by augmenting it.

So Shakespeare had written in *The Rape of Lucrece* (148–54), where lust—a type sin, "including all foul harms" (199)—was defined as the urge to possess something that in the experience inevitably proves mere loss, an overreaching into insubstantiality and negation. In *Macbeth* the positives so securely established—the assured intimation of "the things we [sc., truly] are"—throw into relief, and so sharply define, the defection that occupies the forefront of the play. It is this that makes the play's irony so deeply significant—the irony of making "something nothing by augmenting it," that is, in Banquo's phrase, "by seeking to augment it" (2.1.27); and that central irony of losing in gaining—for Macbeth, like Tarquin, is "A captive victor that hath lost in gain" (*Lucrece,* 730)—lies behind all the often noted dramatic ironies that multiply as the play proceeds. Fear and disorder erupt into the specious security and apparent order that temporarily succeed the murder of Duncan. "Things bad begun" attempt to "make strong themselves by ill," yet each further step is as "tedious" (Macbeth's word) and self-frustrating as the last. And the concomitant of the outer disorder and inner disintegration (with both of which Macbeth identifies himself in the great invocation of chaos in 4.1.) is something that appears to the observer as the betrayal of life to automatism, and within Macbeth's own consciousness as a deepening sense of the loss of significance. It is a radical failure of the human to inhabit his proper world of creative activity. A brief examination of these two related aspects of that failure will conclude our examination of the play's philosophy.

We touch for the last time on the question of "nature." Early in the play we are told of "the merciless Macdonwald" that he is "worthy to be a rebel,"

> for to that
> The multiplying villainies of nature
> Do swarm upon him.
> (1.2.9–12)

Now nature, we have seen, is a power that can be invoked in the service of what is essentially right and wholesome on the sole condition that "human kindness" is recognized as an absolute. Nature by itself, however, is clearly a submoral world, and to "Night's black agents" (3.2.53) in the outer world correspond, within,

> the cursed thoughts that nature
> Gives way to in repose.
> (2.1.8–9)

Man, the inhabitant of two worlds, is free to choose; but if, disregarding the "compunctious visitings of Nature," he chooses "Nature's mischief" (1.5.45, 50), his freedom is impaired. He has "untied the winds" (4.1.52), and the powers of nature enter the human sphere as autonomous agents: in the language of the play, the "villainies of nature" "swarm upon him" as a more or less passive host.

The explanation of this phrase thus involves us in a consideration of one of the main structural lines of the play, where to the creative energy of good—enlisting and controlling nature's powers—is opposed the automatism of evil. To listen to the witches, it is suggested, is like eating "the insane root, that takes the reason prisoner" (1.3.84–85); for Macbeth, in the moment of temptation, "function," or intellectual activity, is "smother'd in surmise"; and everywhere the imagery of darkness suggests not only the absence or withdrawal of light but—"light thickens"—the presence of something positively oppressive and impeding. Both Macbeth and his wife wilfully blind themselves ("Come, thick Night," "Come, seeling Night"), and to the extent that they surrender the characteristically human power of intellectual and moral discernment they themselves become the "prey" of "Night's black agents," of the powers they have deliberately invoked. Automatism is perhaps most obvious in Lady Macbeth's sleepwalking, with its obsessed reliving of the past, but Macbeth also is shown as forfeiting his human freedom and spontaneity. If one ultimate aspect of evil is revealed in Macbeth's invocation of chaos, in his determination to be answered,

> though the treasure
> Of Nature's germens tumble all together,
> Even till destruction sicken,

another is suggested by the banal repetitions of the witches' incantations, the almost mechanical beat in which their charms are "wound up." And just as the widespreading confusion (enacted on the "metaphysical" plane) is reflected in the particular action, so Macbeth's terror-stricken advance in evil is tuned to that monotonous beat. "One feels," says W. C. Curry, "that in proportion as the good in him diminishes, his liberty of free choice is determined more and more by evil inclination and that he cannot choose the better course. Hence we speak of destiny or fate, as if it were some external force or moral order, compelling him against his will to certain destruction." Most readers have felt that after the initial crime there is something compulsive in Macbeth's murders; and at the end, for all his "valiant fury," he is certainly not a free agent. He is like a bear tied to a stake, he says; but it is not only the besieging army that hems him in; he is imprisoned in the world he has made.

It is from within that world that, prompted by the news of his wife's suicide, he speaks his last great speech.

> She should have died hereafter:
> There would have been a time for such a word.—
> To-morrow, and to-morrow, and to-morrow,
> Creeps in this petty pace from day to day,
> To the last syllable of recorded time;
> And all our yesterdays have lighted fools
> The way to dusty death. Out, out, brief candle!
> Life's but a walking shadow; a poor player,
> That struts and frets his hour upon the stage,
> And then is heard no more: it is a tale

> Told by an idiot, full of sound and fury,
> Signifying nothing.
>
> (5.5.17–28)

His wife's death, it has often been observed, means nothing to him. Commentators have been exercised to determine the precise meaning of the words with which he greets it—"She should have died hereafter" (She would have died sometime," or, "Her death should have been deferred to a more peaceable hour"); but the point of the line lies in its ambiguity. Macbeth is groping for meanings, trying to conceive a time when he might have met such a situation with something more than indifference, when death itself might have had a significance it cannot have in the world of mere meaningless repetition that he goes on to evoke. As a final irony this *is* the world where when a thing is done it is merely—"alms for oblivion"—done with, because it is a world devoid of significant relations.

Clearly then we have in this play an answer to Shakespeare's earlier questionings about time's power, as we have also a resolution of his earlier preoccupation with the power of illusion and false appearance. Macbeth *has betrayed himself* to the equivocal and the illusory. So too time appears to him as meaningless repetition because he has turned his back on, has indeed attempted violence on, those values that alone give significance to duration, that in a certain sense make time, for "without the meaning there is no time." He has directed his will to evil, towards something that of its very nature makes for chaos and the abnegation of meaning. The solid natural goods—ranging from food and sleep to the varied mutualities of friendship, service, love—are witnesses to the central paradox of evil, that however terrible its power it can only lead to "nothing."

In the lines,

> it is a tale
> Told by an idiot, full of sound and fury,
> Signifying nothing,

there is combined the apparent force—the sound and fury—and the essential meaninglessness. For Macbeth, now, though in a different sense from when he used the phrase, "nothing is, but what is not."

But the play's last word is not, of course, about evil.

> What's more to do,
> Which would be planted newly with the time,—

As calling home our exil'd friends abroad,
That fled the snares of watchful tyranny;
Producing forth the cruel ministers
Of this dead butcher, and his fiend-like Queen,
Who, as 'tis thought, by self and violent hands
Took off her life;—this, and what needful else
That calls upon us, by the grace of Grace,
We will perform in measure, time, and place.

It is a fitting close for a play in which moral law has been made present to us not as convention or command but as the law of life itself, as that which makes for life, and through which alone man can ground himself on, and therefore in his measure know, reality.

# The Voice in the Sword

*Maynard Mack, Jr.*

In *Richard II,* it is the garden scene (3.4) that catches in an emblem the main issues of the play; in *Hamlet,* it is the chamber scene (also 3.4) with its contrasting portraits of the two kings and the immersing of the hero in the destructive element of guilt; and, in *Macbeth,* it is the banquet scene (again, 3.4). The act and scene numbers of these episodes—garden, chamber, banquet—are, of course, coincidental and critically unimportant, since in most cases our modern divisions come from the First Folio and not from Shakespeare directly, but some such summary and foreshadowing scene at roughly the same point in the play does appear to be a fairly consistent aspect of Shakespeare's tragic orchestration. In this instance, as in the other two plays, we come upon a scene that summarizes clearly the main moral and imaginative issues and foreshadows important developments to come.

Though only one banquet is actually staged in *Macbeth,* the idea and imagery of banqueting are richly developed, as a number of critics have observed, with the result that this scene assumes a significance far surpassing its importance in the plot. The earlier gathering at Duncan's castle at Forres (1.4) had concluded with a reference that associates the mutuality of feasting to the mutuality inherent in any benign social order, where loyalty and gratitude have the importance and almost the palpability of food.

From *Killing the King.* © 1973 by Yale University. Yale University Press, 1973.

> True, worthy Banquo: he is full so valiant,
> And in his commendations I am fed;
> It is a banquet to me.
>
> (1.4.54–56)

Significantly, Macbeth's soliloquy debating the murder of Duncan (1.7.1–28) takes place in the wake of a procession indicated in the folio stage direction as *"Enter, and pass over the stage, a Sewer, and divers Servants with dishes and service."* The contrast between the gregariousness of feasting and the willful solitude of murderous thoughts is thus underlined as Shakespeare frames Macbeth's soliloquy between this procession and Lady Macbeth's entry to say, "He has almost supp'd. Why have you left the chamber?" (1.7.29). Similarly, the massive retaliation of cosmic forces against Macbeth after he has killed his king is foreshadowed immediately after the murder in the famous lines on sleep, also seen in terms of feasting.

> Sleep, that knits up the ravell'd sleave of care,
> The death of each day's life, sore labour's bath,
> Balm of hurt minds, great Nature's second course,
> Chief nourisher in life's feast.
>
> (2.2.36–39)

From the very first, social imagery of banqueting is balanced against actions of anarchic individualism. Duncan's lines about being nourished in and by the commendations of Macbeth follow immediately on Macbeth's "let that be, / Which the eye fears, when it is done, to see" (1.4.52–53). The banquet at Inverness, taking place offstage, as we have seen, is balanced by Macbeth, alone on stage and alienated, considering murder. Likewise, in the banquet scene proper, Macbeth is unable to join the feast because he has cut himself off from the society of mutual trust and obligation that is represented there: first he is prevented by the Murderer's entrance, then by the Ghost's appearance, and finally by his wife, who breaks up the gathering (3.4.117–20). The "broken feast" thus becomes a vivid metaphor of the play's political action to this point and at the same time prepares us for the antifeast of the witches with their "hell-broth" in the next act (4.1.19). Even this perverted "banquet" becomes something like a broken feast as the witches' "gruel" (32) sinks in the cauldron at Macbeth's insistence on certain answers.

What the Gardener in *Richard II* does with his instructions about gardens that are also kingdoms and what Hamlet does with his two lockets (or perhaps merely with a pair of verbal portraits) in his mother's bedroom occurs visually in *Macbeth* when the Murderer enters during the feast. For here on stage before us is a powerful depiction of the antithetical natures of the play's two kings: the feasting fellowship of the lords that looks back to Duncan and the murderous complicity of Macbeth with the Murderer. The Gardener in *Richard II* has to develop the imagery which contrasts Richard with the ideal king, but in *Macbeth* the difference is presented wordlessly. We see suddenly—contraposed—the mutuality of feasting and an obsessive, self-centered appetite no feast can gratify.

Macbeth welcomes his guests, it has been often noticed, in the language of an established order: "You know your own degrees" (3.4.1). The confidence that each man will know his own degree—testimony to an order that is durable and clear—is also testimony in this case to its frailty, since none knows better than Macbeth how easily "degree" can be and has been broken. Underlining this note of irony, Macbeth greets the Murderer not as he greeted his guests, with an insistence on degree, but with an intimation of anarchy: if the assassin has killed Fleance as well as Banquo, he is "the nonpareil" (18). The movement of the scene is thus from the rejection of degree in Macbeth's mind—implicit ever since the first murder and here recapitulated in an attitude that relates it to his rejection of, and also his rejection from, "the good meeting" (108)—to chaos in the company at large. For Lady Macbeth, it will be recalled, is soon to urge the guests to "Stand not upon the order of your going. / But go at once" (118–19), explicitly reversing the terms in which they have been welcomed.

All this is, of course, accentuated in the theater. We are aware, first, of guests taking their accustomed seats at a feast which we realize is essentially a mask for the ultimate breach of degree, regicide. Then there is an interruption by the new king's hired assassin, reporting his murder of one who was both thane and friend, after which the new king, discovering that his place at table has been filled by the murdered man, becomes hysterical. At the end the whole society disintegrates in disorder—although, as we see in the next scene (3.6), the disruption of the banquet signals the emergence of a counterforce that will eventually bring reintegration to Scotland. We have only to suppose, further, that the "state" (5) intended for Macbeth and his lady in this scene is a pair of thrones, one of them being subsequently assumed by Banquo, on his second entrance, to see how much stress is laid here (or is capable theatrically of being laid) on the emptiness of Macbeth's achievement at all levels. He can no more assume the throne than he can maintain a good society. Duncan may be dead in his body natural but in his body politic he yet lives on in Malcolm. Banquo too is dead, but he lives on both as a ghost and in Fleance, whose posterity will be kings.

Another important theme, or pattern of contrasts, to which the banquet scene gives special prominence is that of isolation versus companionship—the solipsism of criminal self-will. Duncan, we recall, is never seen alone; he is always, even in sleep, surrounded by loyal servants. Macbeth's isolation, on the other hand, is intense from the beginning. His progress through the rebel army in act 1 is described as if he were a lonely woodsman cutting through undergrowth (1.2.19), and when at last he slays Macdonwald, his triumph is seen in terms that rather oddly call attention to civilities unindulged:

> he fac'd the slave;
> *Which ne'er shook hands, nor bade farewell to him,*
> Till he unseam'd him from the nave to th' chops.
>
> (1.2.20–22; italics mine)

Immediately upon seeing the witches he retreats into an interior solitude to which Banquo several times draws attention with phrases like "Look, how our partner's rapt" (1.3.143). Later, at Forres, though he is among many, we sense his actual isolation both in his aside about the stars that must not be allowed to see his "black and deep desires" (1.4.51) and in the grim irony of his pledge of loyalty just thirty lines after his "horrible imaginings" (1.3.138) of murder. His benumbed isolation before, during, and right after Duncan's murder is one of the most vivid memories of every spectator, and we can see him in the same abstraction again among the loyal mourners (2.3) after the murder has been discovered. Throughout, except in his earliest scenes with Lady Macbeth, he is spiritually a man apart. Even when with his wife, he seems somewhat isolated by his profounder feelings, and just before the murder of Banquo further sets himself apart: "Be innocent of the knowledge, dearest chuck, / Till thou applaud the deed" (3.2.45–46).

In the banquet scene this all-pervasive alienation receives clear expression in Macbeth's peculiar situation of being alone in company and in company (the company of his wife and the Ghost) when alone. Any echo here of the regal scene at Forres, such as the chair or chairs of state already mentioned, will accentuate yet more the fact that he has brought his isolation from the edge of that scene to the very heart of this one, where (apparently) he never occupies *his* "state" at all. The scene is pivotal, moreover, in that up to this point we have always seen Macbeth alone against the others, whereas here "the others"—first in the form of the Ghost—begin to engage together against him. Soon, in the persons of Lennox (3.4), a Messenger (4.2), Macduff, Siward, and Malcolm (4.3), and nearly all of Scotland (5.2), the balance will shift until all companies and companions are set against the king. Either way he is isolated among crowds, unable to participate at life's feast. The final stage in his spiritual starvation—"I have almost forgot the taste of fears . . . I have supp'd full with horrors" (5.5.9–13)—will recall us to this moment in the banquet scene, and also to that other moment, as he stood withdrawn in his house from another banquet, set for Duncan, when in his hunger for power and security his humanity began to starve. . . .

The morality *Macbeth,* at which we have so far been looking, will not of course do. Macbeth, though a murderer and toward the end something like the monster he is called, is obviously a great deal more than this, as Shakespeare forces us to recognize by means of Malcolm's summary at the play's close: "this dead butcher, and his fiend-like Queen" (5.9.35). We understand why Malcolm and his followers should feel and speak so, and within limits we know them to be right. But only within limits. This is *their* Macbeth; it is not quite ours. Our Macbeth is hero as well as villain, and our response to him is multiple. Though it has been argued that "we cannot adopt [Macbeth] selectively, feel oneness with some parts of him and reject others," I believe this view is unacceptable. True tragic identification seems to require detachment as much as it requires engagement. And in these terms, Macbeth is an extreme and very clear example: our admiration for him is intense but also distant; it is admiration in the word's root sense—a wondering at.

The quality in Macbeth that most engages us is not, I think, his acute imagination, though this has often been proposed. More accurately, it is his deep, almost inarticulate sense of levels beyond our limited experience to which his imagination gives him, and us, some sort of intuitive access. Everything, for the Macbeth of the first two or even three acts, has reverberations, has *mana*. Everything, more-

over, vibrates for him somewhere outside the world of time and beyond the human senses as well as within them, and therefore shakes
him (the phrase is Hamlet's) "with thoughts beyond the reaches of
our souls." For playgoers, probably the best remembered evidence
of this faculty in Macbeth is the murder scene itself, where the reverberations that reach him from the owl, the cricket, the blood, and
the voice crying "Sleep no more" are altogether lost on his wife. She
cuts through the anxieties caused by his inability to say "Amen" and
by his imagined murdering of sleep with the practical advice, "Go,
get some water, / And wash this filthy witness from your hand"
(2.2.45–46). Leaving to return the daggers, she confidently adds,

> If he do bleed,
> I'll gild the faces of the grooms withal,
> For it must seem their guilt.
> (2.2.54–56)

As the assured tone and grim pun on "gilt" suggest, she is unworried
by the blood except as it may be a "witness."

But as soon as she has left, and the knocking offstage has announced, as De Quincey was the first to see, the emergence of some
sort of nemesis from within but also from beyond the temporal, he
looks at his hands uncomprehendingly: "What hands are here?" (58)
and then, in a new key echoes her command.

> Will all great Neptune's ocean wash this blood
> Clean from my hand? No, this my hand will rather
> The multitudinous seas incarnadine,
> Making the green one red.
> (2.2.59–62)

Again her easy literalism is replaced with a wildly imaginative apprehension of a kind of reality in which blood has moral and not simply
literal status. Then this too is set aside by her confident repetition as
she returns from replacing the daggers: "A little water clears us of
this deed: / How easy is it then!" (66–67). We have met with the
washing image before. It occurs at crucial moments in both *Richard
II* and *Hamlet*. Obviously, for Shakespeare it had the usual connec-
tions with Christian purification from sin, but also a special connection with tragic insight. Here, in *Macbeth*, it can hardly be coincidental that the only time we see Lady Macbeth reveal any internal stress
or strain (in the sleepwalking scene) the washing reappears—and in

Macbeth's sense of it: "Out, damned spot! out, I say!"—"What, will these hands ne'er be clean?"—"Here's the smell of the blood still: all the perfumes of Arabia will not sweeten this little hand" (5.1.34–35).

Macbeth's intense consciousness of something that lies beyond the pale of our normal Aristotelian city—where, as Auden says [in "For the Time Being"], "Euclid's geometry / And Newton's mechanics would account for our experience, / And the kitchen table exists because I scrub it"—becomes apparent on our first acquaintance with him.

> If good, why do I yield to that suggestion
> Whose horrid image doth unfix my hair,
> And make my seated heart knock at my ribs,
> Against the use of nature? Present fears
> Are less than horrible imaginings.
> My thought, whose murther yet is but fantastical,
> Shakes so my single state of man,
> That function is smother'd in surmise,
> And nothing is, but what is not.
>
> (1.3.134–42)

These lines are remarkable, as everyone remembers, both for their intuition of some profound inner assault by anarchic forces on his humanity, his "single state of man," and for their apprehension of a buried life within that can under the proper stimulation rise to efface the life of which he is routinely conscious: "And nothing is, but what is not." How far Shakespeare has come in his exploration of the unexplorable may be seen by looking momentarily back to *Hamlet*. The Prince's first soliloquy, like Macbeth's here, immediately opens his character to our view. But there what we see is a man musing on external events in the face of which he must set a clear limit on his actions, "but I must hold my tongue." Here something altogether different happens. As the external reality, Macbeth's new title, Thane of Cawdor, fades almost from his view, his introspections dominate completely—possess him as if he were simply their instrument. It is the difference between thoughts aroused by external and those aroused by internal "events"—thoughts which in fact become their own events. Not his new title but "horrible imaginings" and a "horrid image" take over his consciousness, while out of his internal agitation dawns suddenly the fully developed, if still fantastical, will to murder. There has been nothing to prepare us for this; it seems to be

Shakespeare's way of indicating that some mysterious world and life are carrying on their own business beneath the surface of Macbeth's public character.

The difference between the genesis of the idea of king killing and its genesis in *Hamlet* is also revealing. There, too, the "command" comes suddenly and surprisingly. That something requires revenge is mentioned in the Ghost's sixth line, and the actual command—"Revenge his foul and most unnatural murther"—is our first indication that a crime has been committed. But again the distinction is what matters. Between the external, visible Ghost in *Hamlet* and the mysterious inner impulse in *Macbeth,* the gulf is wide. Even if we argue that Hamlet's Ghost is simply symbolic of his own internal desire and need for vengeance, this must not blind us to the vast difference in tone, dramatic effect, and meaning between hearing a father's ghost command his son to avenge his murder and hearing the will to murder, fully formed in all its horrid particulars, surge up from within. It will not do to say that in *Macbeth* Shakespeare merely does by internal means what in *Hamlet* he does externally, for though this is partly true, the way things are done in the theater is, inevitably, a large part of what they mean.

Macbeth, then, appeals to us, even as he repels us, by his unspoken and perhaps unspeakable intuitions of a life within himself and beyond himself to which we too respond, and tremble as we do. What he experiences seems to go much deeper than the predictable hypocrisies of the villain, whether stage or real. When he participates, for a moment, in Duncan's world, falling into its idiom—"The service and the loyalty I owe, / In doing it, pays itself" (1.4.22–23)—and imaging his duties to Duncan as "children and servants" (25), we have no right to be sure, as too many critics have been, that he is merely hypocritical. Much more plausibly that world is yet a possibility for Macbeth, a potentiality in him, like the valorous service he has just shown in battle against the invaders, the "milk of human kindness" in him to which his wife calls attention, and the scruples that beset him in his soliloquy outside the banqueting chamber at Inverness—not to mention the moral sensitivities that after the murder enable his ears to hear the voice crying sleep no more and his eyes to see the murder sticking to his hands along with the blood. Yet always from somewhere inside him (though also outside him, as the Sisters attest, for they are as visible to us and to Banquo as to him) comes the other urgency, and it floods in now, powerfully, as Duncan speaks to create Malcolm his heir.

> Stars, hide your fires!
> Let not light see my black and deep desires;
> The eye wink at the hand; yet let that be,
> Which the eye fears, when it is done, to see.
>
> (1.4.50–53)

The last line of that passage—which we realize marks some sort of progression in this possession by a life within and yet beyond himself—appropriately hints at a further mystery in his experience to come. For this, though we are only in the fourth scene, is unquestionably the last occasion in the play when Macbeth will be able to refer to a deed done or being done without exciting vibrations in us. Though I think there is much to be said for those who protest the modern tendency to assume that audiences respond to (or even notice) a repetition in the last act of a word used in the first, in some of Shakespeare's plays repetition occurs so insistently and so impressively, that an attentive audience simply cannot miss it. "Honest" in *Othello* and "nothing" in *King Lear* are probably safe examples. So are "deeds," "do," and "done" in *Macbeth*. Not only do these terms pervade the play, but in at least eleven instances they appear emphatically in pairs or triplets and always in striking situations.

> But in a sieve I'll thither sail,
> And like a rat without a tail;
> I'll do, I'll do, and I'll do.
>
> (1.3.8–10)

> thou'dst have, great Glamis,
> That which cries, "Thus thou must do," if thou have it;
> And that which rather thou dost fear to do,
> Than wishest should be done.
>
> (1.5.22–25)

> In every point twice done, and then done double.
>
> (1.6.15)

> If it were done, when 'tis done, then 'twere well
> It were done quickly.
>
> (1.7.1–2)

> I dare do all that may become a man;
> Who dares do more, is none.
>
> (1.7.46–47)

After five such pairings in the first act, the idea of doing and the limits of doing become charged with implication, and in a sense what Shakespeare does thereafter throughout the play is to release this charge at telling moments, most often with ironic force. In the murder scenes, for example:

> I am afraid to think what I have done;
> Look on't agin I dare not.
>
> (2.2.50–51)

In the banquet scene, this theme expands. Macbeth's statement to the Murderer seems to imply a conception of clearly achievable deeds.

> Yet he's good that did the like for Fleance:
> If thou didst it, thou art the nonpareil.
>
> (3.4.17–18)

But then the Ghost's appearance makes him wonder, in lines already quoted, whether nowadays murders can be "perform'd" (76) as they could "i' th' olden time" (74) or whether now the victims always "rise again" (79). By the end of the scene, he seems confident once more that deeds *can* be done, that plans he has "in head . . . will to hand" (138), and concludes ominously, with a loss of insight that we will not appreciate fully till later: "We are yet but young in deed" (143).

In her own less conscious way, Lady Macbeth follows a similar psychic arc, but with one crucial difference. When she comes looking for Macbeth after Banquo's departure on his last journey, she expresses her concern at his recent behavior in the same flat terms she had used in the murder scene.

> How now, my Lord? why do you keep alone,
> Of sorriest fancies your companions making,
> Using those thoughts, which should indeed have died
> With them they think on? Things without all remedy
> Should be without regard: what's done is done.
>
> (3.2.8–12)

Later, during the banquet, she handles the phrase again, quite oblivious to its implication, like a child handling an explosive.

> Why do you make such faces? When all's done,
> You look but on a stool.
>
> (3.4.66–67)

When she uses it for the last time, she will be sleepwalking, reliving forever a murder that in one sense is never "done" and in another even more painful sense is "done" beyond recall.

> To bed, to bed: there's knocking at the gate. Come, come, come, come, give me your hand. What's done cannot be undone. To bed, to bed, to bed.
>
> (5.1.62–65)

An important turning point in the development of Macbeth's character, as I interpret it, occurs in the soliloquy he utters outside the banqueting hall at Inverness, which gives a paradigm in little of his general movement in the play from intense psychic activity in anticipation of an action to the stripping away and narrowing down that every action entails as it creates its own devouring vortex.

> If it were done, when 'tis done, then 'twere well
> It were done quickly: if th' assassination
> Could trammel up the consequence, and catch
> With his surcease success; that but this blow
> Might be the be-all and the end-all—here,
> But here, upon this bank and shoal of time,
> We'd jump the life to come.
>
> (1.7.1–7)

The metaphysical uneasiness that becomes explicit here has been gestating since the opening lines, when a battle could be "lost and won." The ambiguities are in neither case merely linguistic; it is not merely a matter of a battle lost by one and won by another, though that happens, or of a deed not being finished when it appears complete. The ambiguity goes deeper, is metaphysical, even supernatural. Macbeth both wins that battle in act 1 and, by winning, loses— because of the temptations his victory and honors bring him. Likewise, he contemplates in the soliloquy the gap between the performance of a deed and its consequences as a deed performed, but soon all deeds begin to show an ultimate incompleteness. Murders require further murders, and dead men rise. His world increasingly reveals itself as a place in which no settled definitions of man exist, no final deeds, done and over with. It manifests its unpredictableness at every turn, in crises and in trifles—as when Banquo asks the witches, "are you aught / That man may question?" (1.3.42–43), or when the Porter talks about drink's ambiguous effects on deeds, "it provokes the desire, but it takes away the performance" (2.3.29–30). Behind the solid front of Scottish politics, even behind murder and its discovery, we sense that something yet more momentous stirs.

In this soliloquy outside his banquet hall, Macbeth manages to meditate his way out of murder, only to be shamed back into it by his wife's "When you durst do it, then you were a man" (1.7.49). His own earlier demurrer—"I dare do all that may become a man" (46)—a demurrer springing from a still complex awareness of all that it requires to be human—shrinks in just thirty lines, under her prodding, to signify solely courage: "thy undaunted mettle should compose / Nothing but males" (74–75). What the rest of the play then offers in Macbeth's character is an uneven but continuing retrogression from the earlier full awareness to a condition in which all faculties are attenuated to a male and murderous courage, noble and admirable only as the beast of prey is noble and admirable. Macbeth's tragedy, in short, as this soliloquy shows us, is of decreasing internal awareness, and this is what sets him so clearly apart from Richard II and Hamlet, and most other Shakespearean heroes.

The dagger soliloquy follows in 2.2 and again traces in little Macbeth's decline from his characteristic full awareness to a limitation, almost blindness, self-imposed. First of all it establishes the primacy of the visual sense both in the play and in its hero: "I have thee not, and yet I see thee still" (2.1.35). The dagger is a "fatal vision" (36) and is only seen, not clutched, making the eyes either "the fools o' th' other senses, / Or else worth all the rest" (44–45). In phrase on phrase—"I see thee yet . . . I see thee still . . . to mine eyes" (40–49)—Shakespeare emphasizes the visibility of the dagger, partly, I suppose, because it is the instrument of powers that will repeatedly—with blood, daggers, ghosts, and every insidious form of apparation—work on Macbeth's sight ("But no more sights!" 4.1.155), and partly too because its appearance at this moment defines with characteristic ambiguity (is it in fact "vision" or hallucination?) the complex kinds and sources of experience to which Macbeth as tragic hero is sensitive. The witches were visibly on stage whatever their function symbolically as embodiments of his ambition, and were seen by Banquo; the dagger, though invisible for us and untouchable for him, nevertheless leads toward Duncan's bedroom: "Thou marshall'st me the way that I was going" (42). Evil is allowed a supernatural aggressiveness and reality in this play. It is not the evil masking as good which we saw in Claudius, but an evil that expresses itself openly in visible forms. And yet—Shakespeare habitually taking away most of what he gives—the dagger is and remains invisible to us, and Macbeth himself concludes: "There's no such thing" (47).

Shakespeare handles the rest of the soliloquy in such a way as to make us feel that Macbeth is wiser and more perceptive in seeing the invisible dagger than when he rejects it as unreal. Immediately upon rejecting it, he describes the night.

> Nature seems dead, and wicked dreams abuse
> The curtain'd sleep: Witchcraft celebrates
> Pale Hecate's off'rings; and wither'd Murther,
> Alarum'd by his sentinel, the wolf,
> Whose howl's his watch, thus with his stealthy pace,
> With Tarquin's ravishing strides, towards his design
> Moves like a ghost.
>
> (2.1.50–56)

This is a remarkably vivid evocation of an infernal sympathy between nature, night, and evil. Much more vividly than in *Hamlet,* evil seems here to have its own dominations, thrones, and powers, as in Milton's hell. For though they are only images, a projection of the moral weather Macbeth has inside him, like Duncan's harvest and Banquo's description of Dunsinane as a procreant cradle (1.6.3–10), the black vision does take over the stage, suiting, as Macbeth says, his dark deed and repudiating light—a repudiation intensely dramatic as he dismisses his servant, who bears the only torch. The rejection of light, like the rejection of the earlier multi-consciousness, is affirmed in Macbeth's calm "I go, and it is done" (62). What has happened to the probing mind that wondered *if* deeds were done when done? For the second time we have a hint—though only a hint—that the evocation of an order of evil, a conspiracy of nature, may be simply the other face of a narrowing of awareness, and the rejection of vision and "sights" a simplifying of existential complexity.

This was certainly a possibility hinted at—even more obliquely—in Hamlet's dark speech:

> 'Tis now the very witching time of night,
> When churchyards yawn, and hell itself breathes out
> Contagion to this world; now could I drink hot blood,

> And do such bitter business as the day
> Would quake to look on.
>
> (*Hamlet*, 3.2.407–11)

It will be remembered that this picture of cosmic conspiracy, with its obvious parallels in image and tone to Macbeth's and Lady Macbeth's speeches, immediately preceded Hamlet's dizzyingly rapid double mistake of sparing Claudius by thinking too precisely and cutting down Polonius by not thinking at all. We had watched Hamlet struggle throughout to suit the action to the word, and it seemed that arms were "Black as [their] purpose" and "Thoughts [were] black, hands apt, drugs fit, and time agreeing" (3.2.269) only in plays like "The Murder of Gonzago." In the real world of Elsinore, such sinister harmony was difficult if not impossible to achieve. Here, as Macbeth girds himself for regicide, we are seeing the conspiracy of nature spread like an evil yeast through not only the body natural of its next king but through the whole body politic of Scotland. We saw Richard II turn the traditional sympathy of nature for the king into a similar conspiracy (3.2), but this remained essentially a private, internalizing, imaginative operation marking, if anything, the beginnings of an *increase* in Richard's internal awareness. What makes *Macbeth* such a different kind of play is that the conspiracy view ceases to be the imaginative construct of Hamlet's play or Richard's nightmare and becomes real, filled with blood and a strange dynamic power. We are seeing in graphic detail what Marlowe only symbolized loosely in comic trickery: the world that is bought with the sale of one's soul to the devil.

This experience is further anatomized when, in the next scene, the deed of murder drives Macbeth back to a frenzy of psychic division and wild imagining, contrasted almost favorably with Lady Macbeth's unwavering singleness of being. "Amen" sticks in his throat, a voice cries out his name, his own hands essay to "pluck out mine eyes" (58). Carried on the flood of these mysterious and quasi-supernatural intuitions, some of the referents of the good order do return: "'God bless us'" (26), "the innocent Sleep" (35), "Nature's second course" (38), "life's feast" (39). But they return as realities lost, possibilities cancelled out by the act of killing the king.

The murder scene is, of course, a second important turning point. After this, Macbeth makes no major recovery, though he long retains some residue of the sensibility that was his at the beginning.

At the discovery of the murder, he plays the dull hypocrite with no real flair and is all but discovered. The interest shifts now from questions about the inner meaning of his actions to questions about whether he will succeed. Many of the most interesting elements in the scene—the Porter, Banquo's quiet response, Lady Macbeth's swoon—seem hardly to make contact with his consciousness at all. When he speaks, he speaks like Duncan earlier ("There's no art / To find the mind's construction in the face" 1.4.11–12)—far truer than he knows.

> Had I but died an hour before this chance,
> I had liv'd a blessed time; for, from this instant,
> There's nothing serious in mortality;
> All is but toys: renown, and grace, is dead;
> The wine of life is drawn, and the mere lees
> Is left this vault to brag of.
>
> (2.3.91–96)

We recall a time when he *was* capable of balance, as he wrestled with himself the night before, when he asks:

> Who can be wise, amaz'd, temperate and furious,
> Loyal and neutral, in a moment? No man:
> Th' expedition of my violent love
> Outrun the pauser, reason.
>
> (2.3.108–11)

But now, I think for the first time, he sees less than we do. In this too he stands at the opposite pole from Richard and Hamlet, who, though embraced by irony at the start, become less and less open to it as their plays wear on. As Macbeth loses his complex awareness, the audience gains it in a new ironic attitude.

The Macbeth of act 3 is indeed a diminished thing, undergoing what may be called the tyranny of the deed, different from the ambiguity that surrounded action in *Hamlet*—for here the deed performed has achieved a mysterious agent-capacity of its own. What Macbeth contemplated as a metaphysical problem, "If it were done . . . ," now returns to hound him as an inescapable task and reality. In *Hamlet,* the Ghost called for blood; here, blood itself will have blood, the deed done will have another deed.

The direction in which Macbeth is now so clearly heading is emphasized after Banquo's departure in 3.1, in a soliloquy whose details ideally should be compared, item for item, with those which occupied Macbeth's mind during the banquet at Inverness (1.7.). Suffice it to point out, in lieu of such comparison, that though something of the old language persists, it is now sung to another tune. Where formerly we had the baroque energy of "angels, trumpet-tongu'd," and "Pity, like a naked new-born babe, / Striding the blast," and "heaven's Cherubins hors'd / Upon the sightless couriers of the air" to "blow the horrid deed in every eye" (the imagery, unlimited and uninhibited, of a free imagination), we have now the constraining pressures of the practical and expedient—what must be done because something else was done and cannot be undone.

> To be thus is nothing, but to be safely thus:
> Our fears in Banquo
> Stick deep, and in his royalty of nature
> Reigns that which would be fear'd; 'tis much he dares;
> And, to that dauntless temper of his mind,
> He hath a wisdom that doth guide his valour
> To act in safety. There is none but he
> Whose being I do fear: and under him
> My Genius is rebuk'd; as, it is said,
> Mark Antony's was by Caesar. He chid the Sisters,
> When first they put the name of King upon me,
> And bade them speak to him; then, prophet-like,
> They hail'd him father to a line of kings:
> Upon my head they plac'd a fruitless crown,
> And put a barren sceptre in my gripe,
> Thence to be wrench'd with an unlineal hand,
> No son of mine succeeding. If't be so,
> For Banquo's issue have I fil'd my mind;
> From them the gracious Duncan have I murther'd;
> Put rancours in the vessel of my peace,
> Only for them; and mine eternal jewel
> Given to the common Enemy of man,
> To make them kings, to seed of Banquo kings!
> Rather than so, come, fate, into the list,
> And champion me to th' utterance!

(3.1.48–71)

Even the reference to "the vessel of my peace" and "mine eternal jewel"—fragments, we might say, still surviving from the earlier outlook—have become now an argument for more murder to be "safely thus."

We are not, therefore, surprised to find that the conversation with the murderers, which follows immediately, contains nothing that might not have been anticipated of the commonest villain on the Elizabethan stage. As with Bolingbroke, Shakespeare begins increasingly to set ironies at the edges of Macbeth's speeches: when the king claims to have demonstrated Banquo's villainy "To half a soul, to a notion craz'd" (82), he describes better than he intends the sort of person who would murder on the basis of his strained allegations. Even the catalogue of dogs, in its own curious way a reflection of the hierarchical principle that Macbeth has already violated, serves here merely to rate men with beasts and the best men with those who kill best.

When Lady Macbeth enters in the next scene, we realize that the two of them are attuned in a way they have never been before. She echoes the ideas we have just heard him speak in his soliloquy:

> Nought's had, all's spent,
> Where our desire is got without consent:
> 'Tis safer to be that which we destroy,
> Than by destruction dwell in doubtful joy.
> (3.2.4–7)

Her "safer" matches even his "safely." Then, in turn, he echoes her words, though she spoke them before his entrance:

> Better be with the dead,
> Whom we, to gain our peace, have sent to peace,
> Than on the torture of the mind to lie
> In restless ecstasy. Duncan is in his grave;
> After life's fitful fever he sleeps well;
> Treason has done his worst.
> (3.2.19–24)

There is a fitful flash, it may be, of the old distinction between them, she laboring to assure him and herself that "what's done is done" (12) and he realizing that "we have scorch'd the snake, not kill'd it" (13)—but again the intuition of something beyond the mundane and temporal is implicit as this image evaporates under the tyranny of the new deed that he has already implemented. And once more, as earlier in the dagger speech, his mind fills with emblems of a conspiracy in nature which may be the other face of a shrinkage of sensitivity, the fading of his "eternal jewel."

> Come, seeling Night,
> Scarf up the tender eye of pitiful Day,
> And, with thy bloody and invisible hand,
> Cancel, and tear to pieces, that great bond
> Which keeps me pale!—Light thickens; and the crow
> Makes wing to th' rooky wood;
> Good things of Day begin to droop and drowse,
> Whiles Night's black agents to their preys do rouse.
>
> (3.2.46–53)

"That great bond" sounds something like the even-handed Justice, double trust, and golden opinions which defined what a man, and especially a host, should do in 1.7. But, whereas these ideals were there shattered by Lady Macbeth, here Macbeth himself turns the bond into something that merely keeps him "pale." As his more delicate and complex virtues are cut out one by one, the last crude virtues of courage and a desire for clarity increase.

As the focus of the play shifts from what Macbeth thinks and says to what happens to him, our view of him becomes detached, our attitude toward him increasingly ironic. This effect is striking in the scene of his last visit to the Sisters (4.1). Two main elements here compel us to see him in a new light. First, at the opening of the scene, the remarkable increase in seriousness of the witches. For the first time these mysterious creatures sound like true demonic powers as they mix their horrible fragment-feast. Creatures who before had nothing better—or worse—to do than to beg chestnuts from a sailor's wife now speak lines that make the mind recoil, revealing in their conjuration the fragmentation of man and deed, the dismemberment and disjunction of all things, that we have been tracing in Macbeth's interior drama and that set the real nature of Macbeth's murders before us. Whether they have caused or merely reflect these evil actions, the witches introduce a group of images that recall Macbeth's and Lady Macbeth's earlier evocations of a universe of evil and also the murders they have committed.

They announce Macbeth's arrival—"By the pricking of my thumbs, / Something wicked this way comes" (4.1.44–45)—and for the first time, I think, we come close to accepting this as a reasonable judgment. We may still be fascinated by Macbeth's quest for certainty and some horizon where a deed is "done," but we are also increasingly aware of its absurdity. When he asks them what they do, they answer with a phrase that perfectly describes his own doing: "A deed without a name" (49). We have been here before. But now Macbeth insists on finding the deed's name, and for a fourth time his desire to contain and circumscribe what can never be circumscribed and contained ("I am bent to know, / By the worst means, the worst" 3.4.133–34) brings with it images of a conspiring cosmos.

> Though you untie the winds, and let them fight
> Against the Churches; though the yesty waves
> Confound and swallow navigation up;
> Though bladed corn be lodg'd, and trees blown down;
> Though castles topple on their warders' heads;
> Though palaces, and pyramids, do slope
> Their heads to their foundations; though the treasure
> Of Nature's germens tumble all together,
> Even till destruction sicken, answer me
> To what I ask you.
>
> (4.1.52–61)

Here too, as simplicity replaces complexity, chaos replaces the earlier figures of supreme control—the naked newborn infant striding the blast, the "hors'd Cherubins."

A second aspect of the scene that detaches us from Macbeth and envelops him in our irony is Shakespeare's use of the same theatrical conventions he had called on in the dagger speech. There *we* did not see what Macbeth saw—a situation, at that time, of greater mysteriousness than irony. We might have concluded that he was mad, or that he was supernaturally perceptive—but at least he saw more, not less, than we. Furthermore, while vividly describing the dagger, Macbeth himself constantly debated its reality and meaning. We were likely to become engaged with him in contemplating the mystery of this dagger. Here (in 4.1.) Shakespeare exploits our senses in a manner less mysterious than ironic. We hear *and* see the witches' apparitions, whereas Macbeth seems only to hear. Put more accurately—when he looks at the apparitions, he fails to understand what he sees. The apparition that warns, "None of woman born / Shall harm Macbeth" (80–81), is a bloody child, of course related to the babe "from his mother's womb / Untimely ripp'd" (5.8.15–16)—that is to say, to the threat posed by Macduff. Neither we nor Macbeth can at this point know this, but we in the audience should and do note the disparity between the apparition's looks and words. Even a modern high-school audience invariably asks what the bloody child means. The point is that Macbeth does not ask. Where before he found two truths in one experience, the deed that was not done when done, he now leaps anxiously at one truth in two experiences, one verbal, the other visual.

The same thing happens, with an even more mocking irony, in the case of the third apparition—*"a child crowned with a tree in his hand."* Here the verbal message is simply that Macbeth need not fear being vanquished until Birnam Wood shall come to Dunsinane. Again he hears the words but does not sufficiently wonder at what he sees. It does not take a terribly perceptive spectator to suspect that he has just been shown precisely how Birnam Wood *will* come to Dunsinane—as branches in the hands of Malcolm's troops—and to feel accordingly superior to Macbeth. If the spectator happens to remember the vivid image Macbeth himself used after the banquet, "Stones have been known to move, and trees to speak," the effect of detachment will be stronger still. For if ever a tree "spoke," it is the one carried by the crowned child, yet Macbeth does not even suspect what before he knew. The striking character of both images inclines one to believe that Shakespeare intended us to notice a connection and to see in it decisive evidence of Macbeth's waning awareness. In the same way, when Macbeth next says, "Rebellious dead, rise never" (97), he seems not to remember what we recall: that he and we have already seen one dead man rise.

Finally, as if to draw attention to the gap that has opened between a hero who hears only and an audience that both hears and sees, Shakespeare presents a last apparition, who says nothing. It is Banquo, preceded by the *"show of eight Kings."* Our attention is explicitly drawn to the visual nature of this episode: "Show his eyes, and grieve his heart" (110), "Thy crown does sear mine eyeballs . . . Start, eyes! . . . I'll see no more . . . some I see . . . Horrible sight!— Now, I see, 'tis true," (113–22). Forced in this case to understand what he sees, Macbeth becomes angered and rejects everything the witches have shown him—"damn'd all those that trust them!" (139). Our own response to this is likely to distance us still further from Macbeth as we wish he would now "trust them" enough to take their warnings, or had not trusted them in act 1. We still care about Macbeth and wish he would or could save himself, but we are no longer able to overlook the abyss that has opened between ourselves and him.

Appropriately, the scene ends with the play's last extensive exercises on the "deed" that is impossible to be "done." Macbeth's lines here are a remarkable example of how complex a poetry may be written to communicate a diminished and gradually emptying consciousness.

> Time, thou anticipat'st my dread exploits:
> The flighty *purpose* never is o'ertook,
> Unless the *deed* go with it. From this moment,
> The very firstlings of my *heart* shall be
> The firstlings of my *hand*. And even now.
> To crown my *thoughts* with *acts,* be it *thought* and *done:*
> The castle of Macduff I will surprise.
>
> (4.1.144–50; italics mine)

We need not listen very hard to hear echoes here of Hamlet's fourth soliloquy ("How all occasions do inform against me . . .") which worked its way to an equally passionate climax. Hamlet's conclusion, "From this time forth / My thoughts be bloody or be nothing worth," closely parallels in syntax and intensity Macbeth's "From this moment, / The very firstlings of my heart shall be / The firstlings of my hand." But whereas Hamlet speaks of "thoughts" and quietly leaves for England, Macbeth speaks of hands and, immediately after, we see the Macduff family slaughtered.

What Shakespeare seems to be doing here is to recall Macbeth's earlier hesitant meditations by using the same antithetical terms that were characteristic of him then. But now all these antitheses are challenged, not pondered. This is not the man who meditated on the peculiar "undoneness" of things done; this is the language of his wife when she prayed that no natural compunctions should "keep peace" between her fell purpose and its effect (1.5.45–47). At this late point in Macbeth's progress the "deed" is paired with the "purpose," the "hand" with the "heart," "acts" with "thoughts" and "done" with "thought" only that the second of each pair may be surpassed by the first. The full power of a style thick with balancing antitheses is employed, almost paradoxically, to support a narrowing single awareness; complexity exists in the rhetoric but only to be rejected in favor of simplicity in the meaning.

The effects of this deterioration are reflected not only in the bru-

tal killing of the Macduffs, but more subtly in the conversation between Lady Macduff and Rosse (4.2). Under the pressure of fear and
despair Lady Macduff, like Macbeth, uses syntactically balanced
pairs in each of which one term has simply replaced the other:
"When our actions do not, / Our fears do" (4.2.3–4), "All is the fear,
and nothing is the love" (12), "little is the wisdom . . . against all
reason" (13–14). Fear, lack of wisdom—these are the operative motives for her husband's being in England, Lady Macduff argues. Attention is drawn, however, to the one-sidedness of this judgment by
Rosse, who refuses to take her extreme stance, reminding her that
many motives may be involved: "You know not, / Whether it was
his wisdom, or his fear" (4–5). Yet even Rosse has to admit, in a
crowning antithesis that does not differentiate but join: "cruel are the
times, when we are traitors, / And do not know ourselves" (18–19).
Left alone after the messenger's urging to flee, Lady Macduff
wonders:

> Whither should I fly?
> I have done no harm. But I remember now
> I am in this earthly world, where, to do harm
> is often laudable; to do good, sometime
> Accounted dangerous folly.
>
> (4.2.72–76)

She picks up in "harm . . . laudable" and "good . . . folly" the paradoxical antithesis so dominant from the play's first scene. But there
is also here a pathetic Ophelia-like note ("But I remember now") that
sets a human standard by which the ensuing violence can be
measured.

For a whole act after his departure from the witches, we do not
see Macbeth. His absence is even longer than Hamlet's at the same
point in the action and serves a similar function, preparing for the
final confrontation of the hero with his fate. But whereas Hamlet on
reappearance is no less in control of events than before, and far more
in control of his own personality, Macbeth, when he reappears, is
less in control of both. Shakespeare's success is that we keep a por-
tion of our sympathy for Macbeth despite his resemblance to a bear
tied to a stake, for the most part merely reacting to the initiatives of
others.

One of the ways the play achieves this is by the sleepwalking of
Lady Macbeth. Her continuous reliving of the past, her pathetic

wish to be clean of the "spot," her clinging now, when it is too late, to the "light"—all these things remind us of and enact before us a remorse that we may suppose Macbeth (at some subconscious level like this one) shares. And even if we choose not to make the supposition, they move us nonetheless through our memories of a man who murdered at his wife's bidding only to have her, and the deed itself, come to this. We may even choose to believe that awake she is still the brutal force we saw in act 1. But, at the same time—since Shakespeare ever creates double and triple effects—the fact that these visions of blood, ghosts, weakness, and guilt occur in her sleep stresses the deep authenticity of the realities and moral scruples they represent. While, from one point of view, it is only in sleep that Lady Macbeth is weak enough to suffer the pangs of conscience, from another point of view it is only in sleep—sleep which a murder murdered—that such profound moral realities can be faced directly. Lady Macbeth, haunted and probing in her sleep, offers an internal correlative for the counterforces which we have just seen preparing in England.

To take a final look at these forces of reaction, we must first note what there is about them that makes *Macbeth* unique in structure among Shakespeare's plays and what makes the two "plays" we have now discussed into the single tragedy—*Macbeth*. I have traced a progressive narrowing of Macbeth's awareness, a gradual trend toward the simple, external "solution" to what was previously seen as a complex problem with both psychological ("full of scorpions is my mind, dear wife!") and metaphysical ("blood will have blood") dimensions. When we see him again in act 5, he reacts with ferocity to external events, commanding "Bring me no more reports" (5.3.1), exulting in the spoken prophecies of the apparitions, and mercilessly insulting the bringer of news about the English. But in the long scene at the English court (4.3), something new and impressive was added to the play.

In the one aspect of the scene which we passed over before— Macduff's reception of the news of his family's slaughter—Shakespeare momentarily revives the style of complex awareness as he lets us glimpse in Macduff a man who has it in him to develop from the role of messenger into the role of patriot, father, and sympathetic human being, and who can perhaps kill *this* king without repeating Macbeth's act of bloody overreaching. Macduff's reaction to Rosse's news is placed in a context calculated to focus attention on his situation. Earlier in the scene, he has been shown to be brave, loyal, honest. Rosse has described Scotland as a place of sudden death—"good men's lives / Expire before the flowers in their caps" (171–72)—and has called the news he bears so bad that "No mind that's honest / But in it shares some woe" (197–98). Before he has had time to speak, Macduff already senses what is coming—"Humh! I guess at it" (203)—preparing us, I think, for some startling reaction.

The bad news out, Macduff's reaction is startling indeed in its stark simplicity and impressive sincerity: "My children too?" (211), "My wife kill'd too?" (213), "Did you say all?" (217). Though Shakespeare must achieve the effect quickly and by sleight of hand, we are plainly meant to feel that a deep, internal meditation and realization is taking place within Macduff. This in the revenger balances what we saw in the rebel in act 1, when Macbeth suddenly turned inward to his imaginings of murder (1.3.139). In both cases, Shakespeare manages to suggest what he does not actually dramatize—a secret, hidden life of the feelings and the mind.

When Malcolm tries to cheer Macduff, his words are hearty and in the wrong key, the more so as he uses a by now powerfully charged word: "Dispute it like a man" (220). Macduff's answer contrasts radically.

> I shall do so;
> But I must also feel it as a man:
> I cannot but remember such things were,
> That were most precious to me.—Did Heaven look on,
> And would not take their part? Sinful Macduff!
> They were all struck for thee.
>
> (4.3.220–25)

This richly dramatic moment stands out sharply in a scene of ruse, mistrust, charade, and the cataloguing of royal vices and virtues. Here, once again, is the mixed style of double awareness, complicated and genuine. "But I must also feel it as a man": this is the way we wish Macbeth had answered his wife. The "also" is the crucial qualification. Macduff accepts the need for *both* responses, both definitions of man. We feel ourselves, for just a fleeting moment, back with the full consciousness that Macbeth displayed in acts 1 and 2.

Furthermore, we find ourselves back with the modes of thinking that underlay conceptions like the king's two bodies, discussed in the Introduction. Malcolm here urges a response appropriate to the body politic; Macduff agrees but reminds him of the reality and needs of the body natural. The body natural is the flawed part ("Sinful Macduff!"), but it is also the part that excites the most immediate dramatic interest. The good prince cannot afford the luxury of deep feelings, the need for restorative action is too great ("Be this the whetstone of your sword" 228). But his ordinary human supporter and instrument—the good man—can afford to feel deeply, and indeed the play could not afford to be without this moment of anguished silence and sorrowful humility, which matches in the opposing party the subterranean anguish we are soon to see in Lady Macbeth. Many criticisms of the play stem from a belief that Shakespeare has not made enough of these personal feelings—that body natural—in the forces of reaction against Macbeth, and perhaps the criticisms are right.

The last act of *Macbeth* is like a good baroque suite: the interest is less in the richness of any chord than in the way the various voices sound against each other. We see little of the hero, and yet it becomes his tragedy in this act; the morality theme of crime and punishment is worked out, though it remains somewhat external; the most fascinating moments are the glimpses of Macbeth and Lady Macbeth, and yet the play refuses to be seen as a personal tragedy in the same way as *Hamlet* and *Othello*.

As the short scenes follow rapidly on one another, our attention and interest are kept shifting from Macbeth and his wife to their attackers. As I have noted, the scene of Lady Macbeth sleepwalking (5.1) focuses many themes and moods: the horror of the murders, the pitiable internal suffering of the criminals, the way murder "will out" sooner or later, the mysterious resistance to murder even within an ambitious queen. This is followed by a scene that shows us the psychic forces that are internally gnawing at Lady Macbeth, and by extension at Macbeth himself, in their *outward* habit of encounter in the form of the Scottish soldiers under Lennox.

> ANGUS:                Now does he feel
> His secret murthers sticking on his hands;
> How minutely revolts upbraid his faith-breach:
> Those he commands move only in command,
> Nothing in love: now does he feel his title
> Hang loose about him, like a giant's robe
> Upon a dwarfish thief.

MENTETH: Who then shall blame
His pester'd senses to recoil and start,
When all that is within him does condemn
Itself, for being there?

(5.2.16–25)

Set next to this, we encounter Macbeth at Dunsinane reduced to observation of experience rather than reaction to it.

I have liv'd long enough: my way of life
Is fall'n into the sere, the yellow leaf;
And that which should accompany old age,
As honour, love, obedience, troops of friends,
I must not look to have.

(5.3.22–26)

He is now a commenter, no longer a pioneer. The insight remains, but the moral fight is over. The only resistance in him now is outward: "I'll fight, till from my bones my flesh be hack'd" (5.3.32). The Doctor's suggestion that Lady Macbeth's cure is not to be had from medicine but only from within is greeted by Macbeth with "Throw physic to the dogs; I'll none of it" (47). Reversing the Doctor's view, he wants some external nostrum to cure the internal war.

Canst thou not minister to a mind diseas'd,
Pluck from the memory a rooted sorrow,
Raze out the written troubles of the brain,
And with some sweet oblivious antidote
Cleanse the stuff'd bosom of that perilous stuff
Which weighs upon the heart?

(5.3.40–45)

And his conception of the external war is again similarly misguided: "what purgative drug, / Would scour these English hence?" (55–56).

The cure for Scotland will, in fact, be external, because the disease has become external. What began in Macbeth's mind (1.3) has spread throughout his kingdom, as Siward insists, and must be fought there: "Thoughts speculative their unsure hopes relate, / But certain issue strokes must arbitrate" (5.4.19–20). In some ways, this is the heart of Macbeth's tragedy—first that this insight is not his but Siward's; and second that it should come to "strokes." Macbeth has so thoroughly drained himself of *internal* significance that he must be dealt with in the way he dealt with Macdonwald. He will have to be unseamed from the nave to the chops. The psychic and spiritual energy he brought with him has merely festered. It is almost, in fact, as if we have been witnesses to an evolutionary failure: Duncan's singleness of being was replaced with a new capacity for tense, ironic, multiplicity of being, but the new capacity went berserk; its possessor had to be cut down; and the species reverts to something more like the original creature than the deviant. In other words, there is nothing very heartwarming about the forces of reaction in the play. Apart from their motive, which is genuine love of Scotland, they are soldiers who will kill and be killed, like Macbeth. Apart from Macduff, they are impersonal and abstract. We wish them well, but they belong to an emptier world than the one we know.

In our last glimpse of Macbeth before the final battle, we see the man who has emptied that world and, along with it, himself. He is no longer even the Tantalus figure he resembled in acts 3 and 4, when he hoped one murder more would suffice, and would "make assurance double sure" (4.1.83). Now he has fallen away even from that. Like the prisoners in Satan's mouth in the ninth circle of Dante's hell, he is frozen spiritually immobile, eternally trapped. What Dante presents in an allegorical tableau, Shakespeare has shown us happening step by painful step. Before, Macbeth nourished his king and started at his horrible imaginings; now he has "almost forgot the taste of fears" (5.5.9), "Direness . . . Cannot once start [him]" (14–15). He has "supp'd full with horrors," he is all but impervious to the death of his wife, and in the great bleak words that Shakespeare now gives him ("To-morrow, and to-morrow." 19–28), he is the spokesman of all despairs. Appropriately, his dismissal of life as a poor player leads him to the final despair of wishing the whole charade cut short:

> I 'gin to be aweary of the sun,
> And wish th' estate o' th' world were now undone.
>
> (5.5.49–50)

This is quite different from his earlier willingness to see "Nature's germens tumble all together" (4.1.59). That sprang from a frantic interest in his fate, this from a wish to be freed of it.

Challenged directly in 5.6–9, Macbeth recaptures at least a beleaguered animal's activity as he faces his enemies. And it is interesting, I think, that his revival seems to be connected imaginatively with conscious *rejection* of the idea of life as a poor player. The motive behind his resurgent courage in the face of death is clearly shown to be a determination to avoid being merely an "actor" on life's stage. Like Cleopatra, he will not see his greatness buoyed or his nature trivialized by the predictable suicide of the Roman stoic: "Why should I play the Roman fool, and die / On mine own sword? Whiles I see lives, the gashes / Do better upon them" (5.8.1–3). Macduff threatens him,

> Then yield thee, coward,
> And live to be the show and gaze o' th' time:
> We'll have thee, as our rarer monsters are,
> Painted upon a pole, and underwrit,
> "Here may you see the tyrant."
>
> (5.8.23–27)

And he answers:

> I will not yield,
> To kiss the ground before young Malcolm's feet,
> And to be baited with the rabble's curse.
>
> (5.8.27–29)

He will not "perform" either as Roman fool or baited bear. His life may signify nothing, but it will not be that of a player strutting and fretting. Then—the final irony—he storms off fighting with Macduff, an actor after all in Malcolm's revenge play.

On stage now come the smaller, paler figures of Malcolm, Rosse, and Siward. Siward's son, whom we have seen Macbeth cut down like wheat, is found and barely lamented. When Malcolm says, "He's worth more sorrow" (5.9.16), his father fiercely counters, "He's worth no more" (17). We are back in that dry, principled, but not quite fully human world in which York begs for his son's death out of loyalty to the new king. Siward's response seems too unfatherly to be satisfactory. Yet we have just seen in five acts what the opposite of loyalty to the king can lead to. Though neither is reassuring, Siward's loyalty is clearly less horrid than Macbeth's rebellion. This is a tragedy and we are learning what to make of a diminished thing.

Macduff enters the scene of this arid victory with Macbeth's bleeding head. "The time," he says, "is free" (21). But what he carries and what he says do not fit easily together. A huge and bloody price has been paid for this "freedom," and the other freedom that could think of angels trumpet-tongued and Pity striding the blast has been forfeited forever. There is not going to be any satisfying soldier's funeral here, as there was in *Hamlet*. This is a darker, harsher play, despite its greater emphasis on the order which is victorious at the end.

What unites the two "plays" we have traced in *Macbeth*—one of crime and punishment, one of internal awareness—is their common, tragic resolution. Macbeth's degeneration and disintegration are tragic; so, in a different more moralistic way, are his defeat and "punishment." The replacement of nostalgic vision by expedient realism which we noticed in *Richard II* is here changed. Now expedient realism allies itself with representatives of nostalgic vision to destroy the diseased embodiment of a more complex form of consciousness. Structurally, it is as if Claudius were to be allied with old Hamlet against the prince. This structure was latent in *Richard II,* where Bolingbroke was allied with Gaunt as a vigorous leader, as Richard was not. But to a significant degree *Richard II* was, appropriate to a history play, successive in its parts: first, Richard was shown to us in various lights, then he and Bolingbroke collided like mighty opposites, and finally Richard took over the play while losing first the body politic and finally his natural life. *Macbeth's* innovative shape— two simultaneous rather than two successive plays—is the result of moving the "villain" to the center: Bolingbroke and Claudius remain on the fringe. The effect, however, is to make the tragedy darker. Richard II and Hamlet both achieve personal victories as well as genuinely tragic deaths—the old values are at least partially and momentarily restored within them at the end of each play. But in *Macbeth* both "plays" move away from the momentary victory in act 1 when Macbeth rejects the idea of murder. The hero's own awareness *and* the external forces that oppose him move inexorably to the brutal and wholly physical clash that closes act 5. Thus the play concludes on an altogether external note, whereas *Richard II* and *Hamlet* both end with emphasis on the inner precincts of the mind.

Ideal figure, selflessly saving his country, Malcolm begins the last speech of the play by promising rewards to those who support him. This is traditional at the end of tragedy, but it comes as an anticlimax after the horror which we have just seen and which still occupies some corner of the stage in the form of Macbeth's severed head, Malcolm then mentions his projects, "planted newly with the time" (31), and this may carry our minds back to Duncan's trusting plans at Forres. This time the predicted harvest seems more practicable, for we have observed Malcolm's shrewdness, his careful testing of apparently loyal promises, and his effective marshaling of the assault on Macbeth. Still one senses—rightly?—a certain shallowness of comprehension in the lines. No one seems quite to see what we have seen—that weeds grow faster and stronger than flowers, that Macbeth was far worse, but also far greater than any of the survivors. I have referred earlier to Malcolm's summary reference to "this dead butcher, and his fiend-like Queen" (35). If Macbeth is not, as Malcolm thinks, worth more sorrow, he is at least worth more concern. Something great and horrible has happened and something profoundly disturbing in a political sense has been removed. But the profundity of the disturbance in other and more important senses has been ignored. *Macbeth* is a tragedy only for the audience; for the surviving characters it seems to remain a history.

When Macduff at last meets Macbeth, he says to him:

> I have no words;
> My voice is in my sword: thou bloodier villain
> Than terms can give thee out!
>
> (5.8.6–8)

The voice of almost everything human speaks in Macduff's sword, but it is still a sword, and, as such, must forever lack the poet's fully human voice of understanding and sympathy to which we in the audience have been listening. For it is not necessary to sentimentalize Macbeth to perceive what a handful of dust we are left with after he is gone. The new world is ordered, but bare; healthy but bland. Macbeth made himself into a monster, but lived on a level to which no Malcolm or Macduff can attain. The voice in the sword says what must be said, but that does not keep it from adding to the tragedy: blood asks ever for more blood.

Thus there is nothing optimistic about the end of *Macbeth,* but there is nothing pessimistic either. *Macbeth* ends with a restoration of order that is unmatched in fulness and dramatic weight in the other tragedies. Yet no words can quite describe the hard, somber mood of the end of this play. In simplest terms, what has been shown is that killing the king is *almost* inevitably to be attempted and yet is *almost* inevitably unperformable. The king can be killed, but the whole world, human, natural, and supernatural, reacts to offer a new king. Regicide is finally in some strange way impossible, for better and for worse. At a profounder level, what we have been shown is the destruction of a soul, whose intuitions of a life beyond life are his glory and become his ruin; we go from the savageries within a man to the savageries of the battle that cuts him down, from a hero who sees more deeply into the abyss than we do to a villain who, like his opposers, sees far less. Regicide easily becomes a mysterious sort of suicide, spiritual and physical. It is this ironic distance between us and the protagonist and also between us and the antagonists that lends the somber though reassuring tone to the play's end. In Northrop Frye's terms, *Macbeth* is an autumn tragedy heading toward the winter of irony, whereas *Richard II* and *Hamlet* bestride the middle of the tragic spectrum, equidistant from ironic winter and romantic summer.

# A Painted Devil: *Macbeth*

*Howard Felperin*

> *'Tis the eye of childhood*
> *That fears a painted devil.*
> Macbeth, 2.2.53–54

The last of Shakespeare's major tragedies to depend primarily on a native tradition of religious drama is also the most widely and seriously misunderstood in its relation to it. Indeed, *Macbeth* might well appear to be an exception to the principle of Shakespearean revision we have educed from the earlier tragedies. In those plays, the effect of mimetic naturalization over and above the older models contained within them had been achieved precisely by revealing the moral oversimplification of those models, in sum, by problematizing them. But *Macbeth* is unique among the major tragedies in having generated nothing like the central and recurrent problems that have shaped interpretation of *Hamlet, Othello, King Lear,* and even *Antony and Cleopatra.* Certain aspects of the play have of course received more than their share of attention and are continuing matters of debate: the status of its witches and of witchcraft; its topical relation to James I; the authorship of the Hecate scenes, yet these are more pre-critical problems of background and provenance than critical problems as such. For *Macbeth,* as Shakespeare's one "tragedy of damnation," is so widely acknowledged to exist within a relatively familiar dramatic tradition, that critical response to the play has become almost a matter of reflex in assimilating the play to it. This would seem to contra-

From *Shakespearean Representation: Mimesis and Modernity in Elizabethan Tragedy.*
© 1977 by Princeton University Press.

dict the argument so far advanced that Shakespearean tragedy is fundamentally and finally unassimilable to its models, and that this unassimilability is what underlies and generates their problematic status and realistic effect in the first place. At the risk of bringing chaos into order by discovering problems where none have existed, I want now to reexamine the relation between *Macbeth* and its inscribed models in the light of the previous discussion. It may turn out that those models are not quite the ones usually said to lie behind the play, and its relation to them not the clear and settled congruity that it is generally thought to be.

The tradition within which Macbeth is almost universally interpreted is that of orthodox Christian tragedy, the characteristic features of which are already well developed as early as Boccaccio and Lydgate and are familiar to all students of medieval and renaissance literature. It typically presents the fall of a man who may be basically or originally good but is always corruptible through the temptations of the world and his own pride or ambition. This action occurs against the structure of a fundamentally ordered and benevolent universe, which is finally self-restorative despite the evil and chaos temporarily unleashed within it, since crime will [win] out and sin is always repaid. Of course the point in this essentially didactic genre is to illustrate the wages of human wrongdoing and the inexorability of divine purpose. That *Macbeth,* with its malign forces of temptation embodied in the witches, its vacillating but increasingly callous protagonist, and its restorative movement in the figures of Malcolm and Macduff, has affinities with this tradition is obvious and undeniable. The moral pattern of Shakespeare's play is not essentially different from that set forth in Boccaccio and Lydgate, and there is no lack of more immediate versions of it with which Shakespeare would have been well acquainted. He had drawn on *A Mirror for Magistrates* in previous histories and tragedies; several sixteenth-century moralities deal with the same theme; and the same pattern, though without political overtones, informs *Doctor Faustus,* a play with which *Macbeth* is often compared. Shakespeare's own early Marlovian monodrama, *Richard III,* falls squarely within this tradition of Christian tragedy, and its similarities with *Macbeth* were pointed out as far back as the eighteenth century.

Yet there is another dramatic tradition at work within *Macbeth* or, more accurately, a subgenre of this same tradition, that is at once much older than these examples and more immediately and concretely present within the play. For here, as in *Hamlet,* Shakespeare allows the primary model for his own action to remain at least partly in view. We have already seen how the cry of the elder Hamlet's ghost to "remember me" is more than a reminder to his son to avenge his death; it simultaneously conjures up the older mode of being and acting which would make revenge possible, which the action of *Hamlet* at once repeats and supersedes, and which points with all the intentionality and ambiguity of any sign toward the heart of the play's meaning. In *Macbeth,* too, the persistence of an older dramatic mode within the world of Shakespeare's play is no less explicitly recalled. Though there are many places in *Macbeth* that could serve as an entry into this older world, the two modern scholars who have consciously perceived its existence have both entered it through, so to speak, its front door, the "hell-gate" of Inverness with its attendant "devil-porter." For here too the purpose of the Porter's request, "I pray you remember the porter" (2.3.22), is more than to extract a tip from Macduff whom he has just admitted. The reference of his remark is ambiguous, as Glynne Wickham observes, "for it can be addressed by the actor both to Macduff and to the audience. As in the porter's dream, it is in two worlds at once; that of Macbeth's castle and that of another scene from another play which has just been recalled for the audience and which the author wants them to remember."

That other play, which Wickham advances as Shakespeare's "model for the particular form in which he chose to cast act 2, scene 3, of *Macbeth,* and possibly for the play as a whole," is *The Harrowing of Hell* in the medieval English mystery cycles. Derived from the apocryphal *Gospel of Nicodemus* and adapted in two of the oldest rituals of the Roman Catholic liturgy, it is enacted in all of the extant cycles, though details of staging and dialogue differ from one to another. Between his crucifixion and resurrection, Christ comes to hell (represented as a castle on the medieval stage) and demands of Lucifer the release of the souls of the prophets and patriarchs. In all versions, the arrival of Christ is heralded by strange noises in the air and thunderous knocking at the castle gates. In the York and Towneley plays, the gate of hell has a porter appropriately named Rybald, a comic devil who breaks the news to Beelzebub of Christ's arrival and questions David and Christ himself as to his identity. Finally, Jesus breaks down the gate of hell, routs the resisting devils and, after a debate with Satan, who tries to deny the prophecies of his godhead, releases the prophets amid prayers and rejoicing. The Coventry version of the playlet, the one that Shakespeare is almost certain to have seen, is not extant, but there is no reason to think it was substantially different from the other versions. In fact, the Pardoner in John Heywood's *The Foure PP* (1529?), is described as having been on easy terms with "the devyll that kept the gate," since he had "oft in the play of Corpus Christi . . . played the devyll at Coventry," and is himself addressed as "Good mayster porter." With its castle setting, bumbling porter named Rybald, "*Clamor vel sonitus materialis magnus*" in the depth of night, and background of prophecy, the cyclic play of the Harrowing of Hell would have been easily evoked by the business of *Macbeth*, 2.3, in the minds of many in Shakespeare's audience who still remembered the porter. Moreover, the memory of the old play would strongly foreshadow the outcome of *Macbeth* as well, since Christ's entry into and deliverance of the castle of hell also looks forward to Macduff's second entry into Macbeth's castle and triumph over the demonic Macbeth at the end of the play.

Though prefiguring the didactic superplot or counterplot of Macduff's liberation of Scotland and defeat of Macbeth, however, *The Harrowing of Hell* has little direct bearing on the main or central action of Macbeth's personal destiny within the play, aside from rather broadly associating him with Beelzebub or Satan. But there is another play, or rather pair of plays, in the mystery cycles that supply what *The Harrowing of Hell* leaves out in the action of *Macbeth,* namely *The Visit of the Magi* and *The Massacre of the Innocents.* The cycles are more varied in their dramatization of these episodes from St. Matthew than they are in the case of the deliverance from hell, particularly as to the outcome of the massacre, but all share certain elements that bear directly on Macbeth's career. In all of them, three wise men come to pay homage to a king born in Israel and descended from David, the prophecies of whose birth they rehearse to Herod. Outraged at these prophecies of a king not descended from him, which are confirmed by his own biblical interpreters, Herod plans to murder the magi and all the children of Israel. The magi escape, warned by an angel, whereupon Herod sends his soldiers out to exterminate his rival, who also escapes into Egypt. The outcome of Herod's brutality—the murders are carried out on stage amid the pleas and lamentation of the mothers—though different in each version, is in all cases heavy with dramatic irony. The Towneley play, for example, concludes with a self-deluded Herod proclaiming that "Now in pease may I stand / I thank the Mahowne!" In the York and

Coventry versions, the irony is more explicit, as the soldiers of the former admit under questioning that they are not sure whether Jesus was among the "brats" they have murdered, and in the latter a Messenger informs Herod that "All thy dedis ys cum to noght; / This chyld ys gone in-to Eygipte to dwell." In the Chester play, Herod's own son is murdered by his soldiers while in the care of one of the women. When told the news, Herod dies in a paroxysm of rage and is carried off to hell by devils. Even more pointed and ironic is the *Ludus Coventriae* version, in which Herod stages a feast to celebrate the successful execution of his plan to consolidate his reign and succession. Its mirth and minstrelsy are interrupted with the stage-direction, "*Hic dum* [the minstrels] *buccinant mors interficiat herodem et duos milites subito et diabolus recipiat eos.*" While the devil drags Herod away, the spectral figure of Death, "nakyd and pore of array" closes the play with the inevitable moral: "I come sodeynly with-in a stownde / me with-stande may no castle / my jurnay wyl I spede."

The appearance of death at Herod's feast cannot help but recall the appearance of Banquo's ghost at Macbeth's feast. For even though this motif of death at the feast of life occurs only in this one version of the Herod plays, it is a medieval topos which must have been available to Shakespeare from other dramatic or pictorial sources, if not from this particular play, since he had already employed it in Fortinbras' image at the end of *Hamlet:*

> O proud Death,
> What feast is toward in thine eternal cell,
> That thou so many princes at a shot
> So bloodily hast struck?
>
> (5.2.353–6)

Indeed, the influence of the medieval cycles on *Macbeth* is not confined to the pair of plays already discussed but can be traced to other plays within the same cycles. Shakespeare's choric trio of witches, for example, are anticipated not only by the three kings in *The Adoration of the Magi,* but by the three shepherds and the three prophets in the play that precedes it in the Coventry and other cycles, *The Adoration of the Shepherds.* There, both the shepherds and the prophets are granted foreknowledge of Christ's birth, both discuss his prophesied kingship, and in the Chester version, both employ a form of paradoxical salutation similar to that of Shakespeare's witches:

PRIMUS PASTOR: Haile, King of heaven so hy, born in a Cribbe!
SECUNDUS PASTOR: Haile the, Emperour of hell, and of
    heaven als!
TERTIUS PASTOR: Haile, prynce withouthen peere, that
    mankind shall releeve!

Moreover, prophecies of the birth of a potentially subversive child trouble not only Herod, but both Pharaoh and Caesar Augustus before him in the Towneley cycle. Both follow the same, self-defeating course of attempting to defy the prophecies through promiscuous slaughter. Certain details of the Towneley play of Pharaoh may even find their way, from this or other versions of the story, into some of Macbeth's most famous language and imagery. His miraculous lines on how "this my hand / Will rather the multitudinous seas incarnadine, / Making the green one red" (2.2.60–62) may well have their humble beginning in the reported outcome of Pharaoh's equivocations with Moses, the first of Egypt's plagues:

> Syr, the Waters that were ordand
> for men and bestis foyde,
>     Thrugh outt all egypt land,
>     ar turnyd into reede-bloyde.

Or Macbeth's anguished outcry, "O, full of scorpions is my mind, dear wife!" (3.1.36) may echo the same soldier's account of the third plague while internalizing it: "Greatte mystis [of gnats], sir, there is both morn and noyn, / byte us full bytterly." Even the plague of darkness may contain the hint for the dominant imagery of Shakespeare's play. It is not my intention to press these parallels as literal "sources," but it is important to recognize the close affinities of *Macbeth* with a series of biblical tyrant plays, all repeating essentially the same story, each of whose protagonists—Satan, Pharaoh, Caesar, Herod—is a type of tyranny within a providential scheme of history. The apparently innocent request to "remember the porter" opens up an historical context for *Macbeth* that we have only begun to explore.

What, then, is the significance of these largely neglected models as they are deliberately recalled within Shakespeare's play? Glynne Wickham sums up their contribution to *Macbeth* as follows:

> The essentials that he drew from the play [of Herod] are
> the poisoning of a tyrant's peace of mind by the prophecy
> of a rival destined to eclipse him, the attempt to forestall

that prophecy by the hiring of assassins to murder all potential rivals and the final overthrow and damnation of the
tyrant. . . . Like Herod with the Magi, Macbeth adopts a
twofold plan. He aims first at Banquo and Fleance; and,
when this plan miscarries, he extends his net to cover all
potential rivals and strikes down Lady Macduff and her
children. The last twenty lines of this scene are imbued
with the sharpest possible verbal, visual and emotional
echoes of the horrific scene in Bethlehem. Young Siward's
image of Macbeth as both tyrant and devil in act 5, scene
7, recalls the drunken devil-porter of act 2, scene 3, and
thereby the two complementary images of the religious
stage, Herod the tyrant and the Harrowing of Hell, are
linked to one another in compressed form to provide the
thematic sub-text of this Scottish tragedy. Pride and ambition breed tyranny: tyranny breeds violence, a child
born of fear and power: but tyrants are by their very nature
Lucifer's children and not God's, and as such they are
damned. As Christ harrowed Hell and released Adam
from Satan's dominion, so afflicted subjects of mortal tyranny will find a champion who will release them from fear
and bondage. This Macduff does for Scotland.

The passage is worth quoting at such length because it so accurately
reflects not only the indisputable elements Shakespeare takes over in
*Macbeth* from the medieval tyrant plays but the doctrinal message
those plays were designed to illustrate and inculcate, a moral orien-
tation that critics much less conscious of dramatic traditions and
much more "modern" and secular in outlook than Wickham also
find in *Macbeth*. But to assimilate the meaning of *Macbeth* to that of
its medieval models, as Wickham and most other critics of the play
more or less explicitly do, is not only to make Shakespeare's play less
interesting than it is but to make it say something it does not say.
Such an interpretive stance is based on a misunderstanding of the
way any truly great writer uses his sources and models, as well as the
way Shakespeare used his own in this play.

For the resemblances of plot structure, characterization, even
language between *Macbeth* and the medieval cycle plays cannot
simply be ascribed to a pious attitude and a parallel intent on Shakespeare's part in relation to his models. All these resemblances arise in

the first place as a result of the efforts of characters within the work to turn the action in which they are involved toward or even into a certain kind of older action, to recreate their experience in the image of certain precedents for their own purposes, purposes which cannot be immediately identified with the author's and which the play as a whole may not ratify. We have already seen this impulse at play within *Hamlet* and the previous tragedies, where Hamlet, Othello, and Lear all attempt and fail to turn the action into a version of the morality play, and it is no less present and pervasive in *Macbeth,* though here the particular medieval convention involved is a somewhat different one. For from the inception of the Scottish counterplot, Malcolm, Macduff, and the others are given to re-creating present history in terms of medieval dramatic conventions. In Malcolm's depiction of him during the interlude at the English court, for example, Edward the Confessor is presented not as an historical monarch but as a type of royal saintliness, the dispenser of "The healing benediction" and possessor of "a heavenly gift of prophecy" (4.3.156–58). In contrast to the England blessed with such a king, Scotland has become, in Ross's account, a place "Where sighs and groans, and shrieks that rent the air, / Are made, not marked; where violent sorrow seems / A modern ecstasy (4.3.168–70), that is, a hell on earth that cries out for the harrowing. Its ruler becomes, in Macduff's words, "Devilish Macbeth," "this fiend of Scotland" than whom "Not in the legions / Of horrid hell can come a devil more damned" (4.3.55–56). In the same highly stylized and archaic vein, Malcolm proceeds to characterize himself, first as a walking abstract and brief chronicle of vices exceeding even those of the collective portrait of Macbeth, and then as an equally abstract model of virtue allied to Edward the Confessor. To seek some naturalistic basis for his highly abstract "testing" of Macduff is futile, for like Hamlet's "portrait-test," its rhetorical and theatrical overdetermination will always be in excess of any personal motive that can be offered in so far as it is inspired by old plays rather than present feeling. Malcolm, like Hamlet, must go out of his way to abstract and depersonalize himself and his world as a necessary prelude to the scenario of redress being contemplated. He and his fellows must remake Scottish history into moral allegory, thereby legitimating themselves and their historical cause by assimilating them to an absolute and timeless struggle of good against evil. Malcolm and his party must, in sum, represent themselves and their world, in precisely the terms of the play's medieval models, that is, in the name of all that is holy.

This effort to abstract themselves to older and purer roles, however, is not the exclusive prerogative of the angelic party of Malcolm and his followers and not confined to the Scottish superplot. A complementary but antithetical project is already underway near the beginning of the play in Lady Macbeth's attempt to become one with a demonic role:

> Come, you spirits
> That tend on mortal thoughts, unsex me here,
> And fill me from the crown to the toe top-full
> Of direst cruelty. Make thick my blood;
> Stop up th' access and passage to remorse,
> That no compunctious visitings of nature
> Shake my fell purpose
>
> (1.4.38–44)

Her terrible soliloquy is appropriately cast in the language of the tiring room, as if its speaker were an actress beckoning attendants to costume her and make her up for the part she is about to perform, to "unsex" and depersonalize her into yet a fourth weird sister, even to dehumanize her into the "fiend-like" creature that Malcolm styles her at the end. All her efforts are bent toward making herself into a creature who trades lightly, even whimsically, in evil, and if her soliloquy echoes something of the incantatory tone of the witches' speeches, her utterances surrounding the murder reproduce something of their levity:

> Give me the daggers. The sleeping and the dead
> Are but as pictures. 'Tis the eye of childhood
> That fears a painted devil. If he do bleed,
> I'll gild the faces of the grooms withal,
> For it must seem their guilt.
>
> (2.2.52–56)

Her entire effort of depersonalization lies compressed within the notorious pun: an inner condition of being ("guilt") is to be externalized into sheer theatrical appearance ("gilt"), not simply to transfer it onto others but to empty it of the substance of reality and make it (stage-)manageable. Her repeated assurance that "A little water clears us of this deed" (2.2.66) would similarly transmute the red and real blood of Duncan not simply into gilt but into something as superficial and removable as the Elizabethan equivalent of ketchup or greasepaint: "How easy is it then!" There is bad faith here of course, in so far as her transformation never loses consciousnenss of its own theatricality and thus never becomes complete. She would qualify herself for murder by becoming a devil, but to her devils remain only "painted," thereby disqualifying herself for murder. Lady Macbeth's attempt to theatricalize herself into a callous instrument of darkness and thereby disburden herself of the horror of the time is doomed to break down, largely because it receives no external confirmation or reinforcement from her husband—since role-playing in drama as in culture does not go on in a vacuum—who is constitutionally unable to think of these deeds after these ways.

In contrast to her fragile and ambivalent commitment to a mode of imitation which is expedient, temporary, and only skin-deep, Macbeth's commitment is to a mode of vision in which sign and meaning coincide, role and self are indivisible, and an action is not imitated but accomplished, once and for all time. It is a way of thinking and seeing much closer to that of Macduff, who describes the scene of the murder as "the great doom's image" (2.3.74), than to that of his wife:

> This Duncan
> Hath borne his faculties so meek, hath been
> So clear in his great office, that his virtues
> Will plead like angels, trumpet-tongued against
> The deep damnation of his taking-off;
> And pity, like a naked new-born babe
> Striding the blast, or heaven's cherubin horsed
> Upon the sightless couriers of the air,
> Shall blow the horrid deed in every eye
> That tears shall drown the wind.
>
> (1.7.16–25)

In Macbeth's apocalyptic and allegorical projection of the deed and its consequences, Duncan becomes the Christ-like victim, and Macbeth the Judas-like traitor and Herod-like judge who will himself be judged. With its winds, weeping, pleading, and trumpet-tongued angels, the imagined scene conflates features of several typologically related cycle plays, notably those of the Crucifixion and Last Judgment. Within a mode of vision that blurs distinctions between intent and action, subject and object, illusion and reality, even to contemplate such a deed is to shake and crack the "single state of man" in which role and self were formerly united in the figure of Duncan's trusted defender. "To know my deed," he tells his wife after the murder, "'twere best not know myself" (2.2.72), and for Macbeth the rest of the play is dedicated to assimilating himself to the role he has fully foreseen to replace his old one, to closing any gap that remains between himself and it:

> From this moment
> The very firstlings of my heart shall be
> The firstlings of my hand. And even now,
> To crown my thoughts with acts, be it thought
> and done:
> The castle of Macduff I will surprise,
> Seize upon Fife, give to th' edge o' th' sword
> His wife, his babes
>
> . . . . . . . . . .
> No boasting like a fool;
> This deed I'll do before this purpose cool.
>
> (4.1.146–54)

A new and antithetical unity of being is born. Macbeth expounds and enacts a philosophy of language in relation to action that brings him into line with every previous tyrant of the medieval and Tudor stage. Tamburlaine's insistence on the instantaneous convertibility of his words into deeds is notorious, but the same attitude underlies Cambyses' murderous demonstrations of his omnipotence, as well as the decrees of Pharaoh, Herod, and Caesar that all the children shall be slain and all the world taxed. In each case, the tyrant enacts a demonic parody of the divine power he claims, namely the power to make the word flesh. By the end of his play, Macbeth's assimilation of himself to the dictates of the tyrant's role within the older drama being mounted by Malcolm and Macduff would seem to be complete, their dramatic visions having joined into one.

Given that the Macbeths willingly take on and play out the roles of "butcher" and "fiend-like queen" assigned to them in the apocalyptic history of Scotland according to Malcolm and Macduff, how can we contend that they are anything more than the walking moral emblems that the latter say they are, or that their play is anything essentially different from its medieval models? The answer is already implicit in the nature of their role-playing. For the fact is that, despite the different attitudes they bring to their role-playing and the different outcomes of it, Macbeth and Lady Macbeth both have to strain very hard to play out their respective roles, and neither is completely successful in doing so. Lady Macbeth cannot fully become the fiend she tries to be, and Macbeth cannot fully become the strutting and fretting Herod he thinks he is. In the case of Lady Macbeth, her eventual madness is the index of the very humanity she would negate by turning herself into a pure and untrammeled role, the residue of an untransmuted humanity that had sought boldness in drink and was checked by remembered filial ties before performing the act that should have been second nature. Madness in Shakespeare's tragedies always attests to the incompleteness of an unreinforced role-playing, that technique by which the self in its naked frailty seeks refuge from the anxiety of such extreme and disruptive actions as revenge, regicide, or abdication through the adoption of an older and simpler mode of being. In this respect, the "antic disposition" of Hamlet, the madness of Lear on the heath, and now the quiet somnambulism of Lady Macbeth are very different from the behavior of Herod, who "ragis in the pagond and in the street also" when he fails to find confirmation of his absolute kingship in the prophecies, the wise men, and events themselves. For Herod does not and cannot *go* mad; he *is* mad. His "rage" is his role, and no matter how often he is traumatized, he will rebound with cartoon-like resiliency to his former outline, and rage again.

To define the truer madness that occurs in Shakespeare's tragedies, however: what is it but to be something other than role? Those who would follow Malcolm, Macduff, and the rest in equating Lady Macbeth with her fiend-like role and Macbeth with his role of butchering tyrant, and proceed to moralize or patronize them accordingly, are simply not listening:

> MACDUFF:          Turn, hellhound, turn!
> MACBETH: Of all men else I have avoided thee,
>   But get thee back! My soul is too much charged
>   With blood of thine already.
>
> (5.7.3–6)

Macduff's challenge proceeds programmatically out of his own role of missionary, Christ-like avenger. Yet Macbeth's response proceeds not out of his assigned and chosen role of stage-tyrant, but out of an unsuspected reserve of sympathetic and spontaneous humanity that exists beneath it, a self still fragile and unhardened in evil even at this point, against his own and Macduff's protestations and accusations to the contrary. And Shakespeare's juxtaposition of the two reveals how inadequate and inappropriate are the moral terms deriving from the didactic drama of Satan, Pharaoh, Herod, Cambyses, even Richard III, to the drama of Macbeth.

Shakespeare makes it clear that Macbeth's play is in a fundamental sense *not* their play, despite the efforts of the characters within it, including Macbeth, to conform it to an orthodox tyrant play, and the many resemblances that result. Consider, for example, the nature of the prophecies and the manner in which they are accomplished. Just as Herod had questioned the Magi (and in one version his own interpreters), Macbeth questions the Witches. He is shown in a highly archaic dumb show an emblem of a "Child Crowned, with a tree in his hand" and another of a "Bloody Child," with accompanying glosses to the effect that "none of woman born / Shall harm Macbeth" and "Macbeth shall never vanquished be until / Great Birnam Wood to high Dunsinane Hill / Shall come against him" (4.1.80–91, 92–94). Malcolm's camouflaging of his troops with the foliage of Birnam Wood identifies him with the crowned child bearing a branch, Macduff's Caesarean birth identifies him with the bloody child, and together they do indeed overcome Macbeth, with all the irony of a violated nature having her vengeance on the man who has violated her workings in himself. Yet even as these prophecies come true, they do so with an air of contrivance and artificiality quite alien to the inevitability of those of the cycle plays. On the religious stage the prophecies had had a literal transparency that those of *Macbeth* no longer possess. No interpretive effort is necessary to reconcile what was predicted (a king is to be born who will supplant Herod) and what occurred; or the literal meaning of the prophecy (Christ will supplant Herod) and its moral meaning (good will supplant evil); or the signs in which the prophecy is expressed (a star in the sky like a "sun"; a word in a sacred text) and their significance (the "son" of God, the "word made flesh").

In *Macbeth,* by contrast; a strenuous interpretive effort is necessary to reconcile the portentous emblems and pronouncements of the witches' dumb show with their human and natural fulfillments, though we are largely unconscious of that effort when we make it. This is not simply a matter of the trickiness traditionally associated with prophecies of demonic origin. For not only are the prophecies of *Macbeth* not transparent and univocal as the prophecies of the Herod plays had been; strictly speaking, they do not even come true.

It is not Birnam Wood but Malcolm's army bearing branches from Birnam Wood that comes against Macbeth at Dunsinane. Macduff may have been "Untimely ripped" from his mother's womb, making him something of a man apart, but that hardly qualifies him as one not "of woman born," the immaculate and otherworldly avenger of a fallen Scotland. It is only when we suppress their literal meaning (and our own literalism) and take the prophecies solely at a figurative level that they can be said to "come true" at all, let alone be made to illustrate the kind of moral logic we like to read out of them. In his handling of the prophecies so as to reveal their "double sense," their disjuncture of literal and figurative meanings, Shakespeare has introduced an element of parody, of fallen repetition, into his play in relation to its medieval models.

Yet this parodic discrepancy between Christian vision and Shakespearean revision which runs through the play does not in the least prevent the Scottish resurgents from blithely conducting themselves and their counterplot as if no such gap existed and the two were one and the same, even though their own elected roles and exalted design are compromised by it. We might think, for example, that Macduff's unexplained abandonment of his own children and wife to Macbeth's tyranny, though ultimately providing him with the most natural of motives for revenge, could scarcely strengthen his claim to the exalted, impersonal role of Scotland's avenger prescribed by the play's Christian model. After all, even on the medieval stage it is the epic, superhuman Christ of the Apocalypse who harrows hell, and not the more human figure of the gospels. But for the Scottish resurgents, these deeds must not be thought of after these ways. It is precisely their capacity to sublimate their naked frailties into the service of a missionary role and a divine plan that constitutes their real strength and the prerequisite for their success. Macduff's personal guilt and grief are instantly transformed, at Malcolm's prompting, into the "whetstone" of his sword in the impending divine conflict, for which "the pow'rs above / Put on their instruments" (4.3.238–49). As such an "instrument" of righteousness, Macduff "wants the natural touch" (4.2.9) in more ways than his wife imagines. His unhesitating absorption into his role is never more astonishing than when he finally presents his own nativity legend, however literally lacking it may be, as the necessary credential for defeating Macbeth, however invincible in combat he once again appears. The same absence of self-doubt or self-consciousness in his new kingly role also characterizes Malcolm (whose single act prior to the mounting of the counterplot was also one of flight), particularly in his disposition of that "which would be planted newly with the time" (5.8.65) after the final victory. His announced intent of rewarding his followers with promotion to the rank of earl and of punishing his foes ("The cruel ministers / Of this dead butcher and his fiend-like queen" [5.8.68–69]) sets the seal on the new historical order of his reign as a secular imitation of divine judgment. Yet the scene is also an eerie and unsettling repetition of an earlier scene in the play. For Malcolm's language and gestures cannot help but recall those of Duncan after the victory over Cawdor and Macdonwald, a new era of freedom and love that proved only too fragile and temporary, anything but an apocalyptic triumph of good over evil. The battle toward a civilized and humane order, like all the play's battles would seem only to have been lost and won after all. The arrival of Malcolm and Macduff at Dunsinane is decidedly not the harrowing of hell or the coming of Christ, though its partisans behave as if it were.

Of course it is not really surprising that Macduff and Malcolm never come to perceive, much less feel, themselves to inhabit the gap between the heroic and archaic roles they adopt and the precarious selves that adopt them. For they are ultimately akin to such earlier Shakespearean tragic foils as Laertes and Edgar, unselfconscious and unselfquestioning imitators of an inherited and wholly conventional way of acting, two-dimensional characters in a three-dimensional world. It makes no difference whether we say that such foils seem cardboard or cut-to-pattern because they are supporting actors or that they are doomed to be supporting actors because they are cardboard and cut-to-pattern. For it is precisely the conventionality of Laertes' rant and Edgar's mock-madness that throws into relief the dimensionality of Hamlet's and Lear's more demanding experience. We cannot accept in them an unreflectiveness, even an insensitivity that is harder to accept or understand in Shakespeare's protagonists themselves. We are not unsettled when Laertes acts like Laertes, rants for revenge and leaps into his sister's grave. The cat will mew, the dog will have his day. It is much more unsettling, however, when Hamlet acts like Laertes, betrays the very depth and sensitivity that distinguishes him from Laertes, and does the same. Similarly, no one is shocked when Macduff enters with "the tyrant's cursed head" atop a pike and apocalyptically proclaims that "The time is free" (5.8.55), nor when Malcolm lends his blessing to the deed and the sentiment. For that judicial brutality and the ritual language that surrounds it proceed directly out of the ingenuous repetition of convention that we have come to expect from these characters and violate nothing that has been shown to exist in either of them. Macbeth's brutalities, by contrast, and the self-brutalization that makes them possible are profoundly disturbing to us, not simply because they remain so disturbing to him, and not simply because they represent, as one critic puts it, "murder by thesis"—for what else is Macduff's decapitation of Macbeth?—but because they betray precisely that fullness of humanity with which Shakespeare has endowed *him* in contrast to his foils. In his strenuous effort to become the complete tyrant, to achieve the demonic equivalent of his angelic foils' unselfconscious conventionality, Macbeth must go out of his way to ignore the gap he senses between the pious and preordained view of things and the way things are, must do willfully what the others do quite naturally.

The question arises, then, why does Macbeth accept his destiny as a latter-day Herod, when he is not Herod? For no less remarkable than Macduff's unhesitating conviction that his birth carries the necessary credential for defeating him, is Macbeth's unresisting acceptance of it and the consequent slackening of his "better part of man." Why does Macbeth acquiesce to prophecies that require his cooperation to be fulfilled? The answer to these questions, I would suggest, lies in the mode of vision that we have already seen him bring to his experience before the murder of Duncan. He simply cannot do otherwise, not because his actions are compelled from without—the prophecies are not theologically binding like those of the cycle plays but psychologically self-fulfilling—but because he has long since internalized his society's way of seeing and thinking. Both before and after the murder, Macbeth's is a primitive and animistic world of portents and totems, of stones that "prate" of his whereabouts, of a bell that summons to heaven or hell, of knocking that might raise the dead, of the crow turned emblem of darkness, of night that is synonymous with evil, of accusing voices and menacing visions, a world become archaic melodrama burdened with significance. This "overperception," in which distinctions between subject and object, man and nature, illusion and reality, past and present—all the potential distinctions of our modern critical and historical consciousness—are lost, is characterized in its essence by Lady Macbeth, when she reminds her husband that "'Tis the eye of childhood / That fears a painted devil," that "these flaws and starts . . . would well become / A woman's story at a winter's fire, / Authorized by her grandam" (3.4.63–66). Yet it is just such a childlike and superstitious vision that finally binds everyone else in the play, including Macbeth, into a society as traditional and cohesive as a tribe or a clan. It is the vocation of the ruling and priestly class of such a society to paint, fear, and punish the devils who endanger that cohesiveness and their own power, and this is exactly what the Scottish thanes do, from the suppression of Macdonwald and Cawdor to the overthrow of Macbeth. The act of mounting atop a pole Macdonwald's and Macbeth's painted images, or better still their heads, is necessary as a totemic deterrent to tyranny, a public symbol of the inviolability of the social order and glaring reminder of the inevitability of the moral law that sustains it: the wages of ambition is, and always must be, death. Macbeth had been an integral part of this social order, as Cawdor had been, so it is in no way surprising to see them both attempt to conform their careers to the sacred fictions they were born into and carry around within them. Cawdor by repenting like a morality protagonist and Macbeth by remaining the arch tyrant to the end. Macbeth and Macduff understand one another perfectly, across the moral gulf that separates them, for both speak the primitive language of the tribe.

This is not to suggest that Shakespeare is simply holding up to ridicule the sacred myths, symbols, and forms that so pervade *Macbeth*. It is Marlowe, not Shakespeare, who is given to expressing an adolescent contempt for religion as something invented to "keep men in awe." The play is much more than an easy demystification of the ritual forms that dominate the consciousness and condition the actions of virtually all its principles, for it shows those forms to be at once quite arbitrary and fictive in themselves but wholly necessary and "real" in the social function they serve. In this respect, the play presents a stylization not only of Shakespeare's own society, where these Christian, ritual forms still prevail, but of all societies. It would be the height of ethnocentric naivete to view the "ecstatic" or "nostalgic" community depicted in *Macbeth* as any more primitive in its constitution than later, more "enlightened" societies in which heads are no longer mounted on poles. The gibbet in the eighteenth century—some of whose Shakespearean criticism does indeed condescend to his Elizabethan "barbarism,"—or the electric chair in the twentieth are designed to serve the same necessary function of deterring deviance within the community and to preserve the same necessary fiction that crime must inevitably be followed, as the night the day, by punishment. Moreover, the play depicts the impulse constitutive of every society to makes its particular social forms and institutions, which are always arbitrary insofar as they are manmade, seem as necessary as natural forms and processes themselves, indeed a logical extension of them:

> I have begun to plant thee and will labor
> To make thee full of growing.
>
> (1.4.28–29)

> What's more to do,
> Which would be planted newly with the time—
> As calling home our exiled friends abroad.
>
> (5.8.64–66)

> My way of life
> Is fall'n into the sear, the yellow leaf.
>
> (5.3.22–26)

Within a world that sees itself through the ritual forms of the medieval drama, in which the book of human history and the book of nature are one volume of God's making, it is almost a reflex of all its members to describe the social and historical process of meting out rewards and punishments, for all its demonstrated fallibility, in an imagery of unfailing natural process. But to dismiss this impulse as a version of nostalgic fiction or pathetic fallacy is to misunderstand the play. For like Macbeth's, Duncan's, Lennox's, and the others' investment of the natural world with human attributes, these efforts to endow the human and historical world with a serene inevitability that properly belongs only to nonhuman nature is more than fiction and less than truth, another aspect of the persistent recreation of the sacred, the remystification of the merely secular, that defines the world of the play in its essential doubleness.

It is this radical equivocation of *Macbeth* in relation to its medieval models, the double sense in which it at once recreates those models through the communal effort of its characters and reveals them to be a means of social and institutional legitimation, that makes the play so susceptible to pious mystification or ironic demystification. Of these possibilities for misinterpretation, the pious reading has of course prevailed. The play is generally regarded as a humanization and vivification, through the flesh and blood of Shakespeare's mature language and dramaturgy, of the bare skeleton of its stagy and didactic antecedents. In this view, their homiletic intent though it may be softened is not fundamentally questioned or altered in the process of benign and respectful transformation. The "good" characters are granted just enough of a depth they do not possess, and the "evil" characters are denied just enough of the depth they do possess, to flatten the play into a consistent domestication of a wholly traditional moral design. But surely it must be otherwise, for in what does Shakespeare's humanization of his sources consist but the putting into question of their conventional roles and forms? To the extent that the figures who carry around with them that older moral design as a sacred and unselfconscious trust are made to appear conventional, predictable, and bidimensional by contrast with the figures with whom they share the stage and who are restless in their roles, however strenuously they attempt to conform to them, that older moral design can no longer be authoritative. Critics have always been responsive to the interiority of Macbeth's struggle, but they have been reluctant to recognize that it is achieved precisely at the expense of his status as a moral emblem or example. Yet he becomes something much more interesting to us than any moral emblem in the process, and not because, as the critical commonplace would have it, evil is intrinsically more interesting than good. Macbeth is more interesting than his prototypes and foils, not because they are good and he becomes evil—for Herod is hardly "good"— nor even because they "are" and he "becomes"—for his change is in many ways regressive—but because he cannot take his nature for granted. He cannot quite rest content in an action in which his role and his nature are determined in advance, but must continuously reinvent himself in the process of acting them out. It is in this that Macbeth's "modernity" consists and that his case bears directly on our own, at least to the extent that we are as fully human as he is. In this respect, too, he becomes a very different kind of dramatic model, a type of modernity whose compelling interest for the playwrights who follow Shakespeare will cause him to be imitated again and again.

The simplifications that have become doctrine in the tradition of interpretation of *Macbeth* are the result not only of a failure to establish the play's relation to its models in its full ambivalence, but of a failure to identify the play's primary models in the first place. Just as *Hamlet* has less to do with Senecan revenge drama than with native morality tradition, so *Macbeth* has less to do with the morality play than with the tyrant plays of the biblical cycles. Its nearest contemporary analogue is not Marlow's *Faustus*, with which it is often compared as a parallel study in the psychology of damnation, but *Tamburlaine* or even *Edward II*, those early Elizabethan history plays which, like Macbeth, are modeled on the medieval tyrant plays that are the authentic prototypes of Elizabethan historical tragedy. The morality play is a misleading model in the interpretation of *Macbeth* insofar as it presents a world already more cerebral and voluntaristic than the cultic and animistic world of the cycles. It emphasizes, that is, freedom of moral choice within a mental setting, as opposed to the communal and typological destiny unfolded in the cycles. This misplaced emphasis on moral choice within *Macbeth*, where it receives little of the extended deliberation accorded to it in *Hamlet*, may well arise from the forced imposition of morality conventions upon the play and may well underlie all the misguided adulation of the bland and reticent Banquo and the equally misguided pity for Macbeth. For Macbeth's choices and actions, as I have tried to show, are not free in the way the morality protagonist's are, but are largely determined by his own and his society's expectations soon after the play begins. The universe of *Macbeth* is not ultimately and comically free, as it is even in those variations of the morality (like *Faustus*) where the protagonist persists in choosing wrongly and thus qualifies as an object of tragic pity, but is conditioned by forces largely outside his control. Of course those forces are no longer the benign and providential ones embodied in the figures of God and his angels who descend from above upon the human community below. Rather, they are disruptive forces that periodically and inexplicably bubble up, as it were, from within human nature and society, as the witches who incarnate and herald them seem to do from within the earth itself. Unlike the morality protagonist, who is confronted at all points with a clear choice between moral meanings already established by generations of sophisticated theological apologetics, Macbeth, and the protagonist of Elizabethan historical tragedy generally, must struggle with meaning as it ambiguously unfolds in the world. It is only by confusing these two dramatic modes that such reassuring commonplaces as "the Elizabethan world picture" or "the great chain of being" could misleadingly have been applied as a norm in the interpretation of Shakespeare's histories and tragedies in the first place, as if the "natural condition" they present were order and the life of man could be analogized to the life of nonhuman nature. In our own struggle with the meaning of *Macbeth*, the proper identification of those models actually implicit within the play thus proves crucial and affirms once again the interdependence of literary history and interpretation.

# Two Scenes from *Macbeth*

*Harry Levin*

*Hamlet* without the Prince would still be more of a spectacle than *Macbeth* without the Thane of Glamis. Though the latter is not introspective by nature, his soliloquizing is central to the play, as he considers intentions, casts suspicions, registers hallucinations, coerces his conscience, balances hope against fear, and gives thought to the unspeakable—all this while sustaining the most energetic role in the most intense of Shakespeare's plays. *Macbeth* is the fastest of them, as Coleridge pointed out, while *Hamlet,* at almost twice its length, is the slowest. Thus the uncut *Hamlet* has plenty of room for other well-defined characters and for highly elaborated subplots. Whereas *Macbeth,* which has come down to us in a version stripped for action, concentrates more heavily upon the protagonist. He speaks over thirty percent of the lines; an overwhelming proportion of the rest bear reference to him; and Lady Macbeth has about eleven percent, all of them referring to him directly or indirectly. Most of the other parts get flattened in this process, so that his may stand out in bold relief. Otherwise, as Dr. Johnson commented, there is "no nice discrimination of character." As Macbeth successively murders Duncan, Banquo, and Lady Macduff with her children, a single line of antagonism builds up through Malcom and Fleance to the effectual revenger, Macduff. There is evidence, in the original text and in the subsequent stage-history, to show that the grim spareness of the plot was eked out by additional grotesqueries on the part of the witches.

From *Shakespeare's Craft: Eight Lectures,* edited by Philip H. Highfill, Jr. © 1982 by the George Washington University. Southern Illinois University Press, 1982.

I make this preliminary obeisance to the centrality of the hero-villain because it is not to him that I shall be calling your attention, though it should be evident already that he will be reflected upon by my sidelights. In skipping over the poetry of his speeches or the moral and psychological dimensions of character, I feel somewhat like the visitor to a Gothic edifice whose exclusive focus is devoted to a gargoyle here and there. I should not be doing so if the monument as a whole were less memorably familiar than it is, or if the artistic coherence of a masterpiece did not so frequently reveal itself through the scrutiny of an incidental detail. My two short texts are quite unevenly matched, though not disconnected in the long run. One of them, the Porter's scene, has been regarded more often than not as a mere excrescence or intrusion. The other, the Sleepwalking Scene, has become one of the high spots in the repertory as a set piece for distinguished actresses. The lowest common denominator between them is that both have been written in prose. Apart from more functional purposes, such as documents and announcements, Shakespeare makes use of prose to convey an effect of what Brian Vickers terms "otherness," a different mode of diction from the norm. To cite the clearest instance, Hamlet's normal personality is expressed in blank verse; he falls into prose when he puts on his "antic disposition." This combines, as do the fools' roles, the two major uses of Shakespeare's nonmetrical speech: on the one hand, comedy, low life, oftentimes both; on the other, the language of psychic disturbance.

Our two scenes are enacted in these two modes respectively. But, before we turn to them, let us take a very brief glance at the outdoor stage of the Shakespearean playhouse. On that subject there has been an infinite deal of specific conjecture over a poor halfpenny-worth of reliable documentation, and many of those conjectures have disagreed with one another. Over its most general features, however, there is rough agreement, and that is all we need here. We know that its large jutting platform had a roof supported by two pillars downstage; one of which might conveniently have served as the tree where Orlando hangs his verses in *As You Like It*. We are also aware of an acting space "aloft" at stage rear, whence Juliet or Prospero could have looked down. As for the curtained space beneath, that remains an area of veiled uncertainty. Yet the back wall of the tiring-house had to include an outside doorway big enough to accommodate the inflow and outflow of sizable properties, and possibly to present a more or less literal gate upon due occasion. Hence it is not difficult to conceive of the stage as the courtyard of a castle, into which outsiders would arrive, and off of which branched chambers for the guests, who might hurriedly rush out from them if aroused by some emergency. Moreover, the surrounding auditorium, open to the skies and rising in three tiers of galleries, might itself have presented a kind of courtyard. Not that this arrangement was representational. It was the stylization of the theatrical arena that made possible its scope and adaptability.

Much depended, of course, upon the convention of verbal scenery. When the aged, gracious, and serene King Duncan appears at the gate of Glamis Castle, his introductory words sketch the setting and suggest the atmosphere:

> This castle hath a pleasant seat, the air
> Nimbly and sweetly recommends itself
> Unto our gentle senses.
>
> (1.6.1–3)

The description is amplified by Banquo with his mention of "the temple-haunting marlet," the bird whose presence almost seems to consecrate a church, one of the succession of birds benign and malign whose auspices are continually invoked. The description of the marlet's "procreant cradle" (8)—and procreation is one of the points at issue throughout—assures us that "the heaven's breath / Smells wooingly here" (5,6). And Banquo completes the stage-design:

> Where they most breed and haunt, I have observ'd
> The air is delicate.
>
> (1.6.9–10)

Knowing what we have been informed with regard to Duncan's reception, and what he is so poignantly unaware of, we may well find it a delicate situation. Stressing its contrast to the episodes that precede and follow it, Sir Joshua Reynolds called it "a striking instance of what in painting is termed *repose*." Repose—or rather, the absence of it—is fated to become a major theme of the tragedy. It will mean not rest but restlessness for Macbeth, when Duncan all too soon is accorded his last repose. Are we not much nearer, at this point, to the fumes of hell than to the heaven's breath? Macbeth, as he will recognize in a soliloquy, "should against his murtherer shut the door," rather than hypocritically welcoming Duncan in order to murder him (1.7.15). Duncan has been a ruler who exemplified royalty, a guest who deserved hospitality, and a man of many virtues who has commanded respect, as Macbeth himself acknowledges. The scene is set for the crimes and their consequences by his two-faced welcome into the courtyard of Macbeth's castle.

By the end of the incident-crowded first act, in spite of his hesitant asides and soliloquies, everything has fallen into place for the consummation of the Witches' cackling prophecies. The second act begins ominously with Banquo's muted misgivings; he supplicates the "merciful powers"—who seem less responsive than those darker spirits addressed by Lady Macbeth—to restrain in him "the cursed thoughts that nature / Gives way to in repose," and retires after Macbeth has wished him "Good repose" (2.1.7–9, 29). This exchange would seem to occur in the courtyard, which becomes the base of operations for the murder. The first scene culminates in the vision of the dagger, hypnotically drawing Macbeth to the door of Duncan's quarters. Leaving them after the deed, as he recounts to his wife in the second scene, he has experienced another hallucination: the voice that cried "Sleep no more!" (2.2.32). Meanwhile Lady Macbeth has soliloquized, fortified with drink, and he has cried out offstage at the fatal instant. One residual touch of humanity, the memory of her own father, has inhibited her from killing the king herself; but she is Amazonian enough, taking the bloody daggers from her badly shaken husband with a crude and cruel joke (the pun on "gild" and "guilt"), to reenter the death chamber and plant them upon the sleeping grooms (2.2.53–54). It is then that the tensely whispered colloquies between the guilty couple are suddenly interrupted by that most portentous of sound effects: the knocking at the gate.

This is the point of departure for a well-known essay by Thomas De Quincey, who argues, rather overingeniously, that the interruption helps to restore normality, calming the excited sensibilities of the spectator. "The reaction has commenced; the human has made its reflux upon the fiendish; the pulses of life are beginning to beat again," De Quincey concludes, "The reestablishment of the goings-on of the world in which we live makes us profoundly sensible of the awful parenthesis that had suspended them." Here De Quincey, who elsewhere styled himself "a connoisseur of murder," seems to have got his proportions wrong. Surely it is the Porter's Scene that forms a parenthesis in an increasingly awful train of events. "Every noise appalls me," Macbeth has said (2.2.55). For him—and for us as well—the knock reverberates with the menace of retribution, like the opening notes of Beethoven's Fifth Symphony. It heralds no resumption of diurnal business as usual. Let us bear in mind that the knocker is to be the avenger, the victim who will have suffered most from the tyrant's cruelty. Macduff's quarrel with Macbeth, according to Holinshed's chronicle, first arose because the Thane of Fife did not fully participate when commanded by the King of Scotland to help him build the new castle at Dunsinane. It is surprising that Shakespeare did not utilize that hint of motivation; possibly he did, and the scene was among those lost through the rigors of cutting. It would have added another turn of the screw to Macbeth's seizure of Macduff's castle at Fife and the domestic massacre therein.

As for Dunsinane Castle, it is ironic that Macbeth should count upon its strength and that it should be so easily surrendered, "gently rend'red," after a few alarums and excursions (5.7.24). It comes as a final reversal of the natural order that he, besieged and bound in, should be assaulted and overcome by what appears to be a walking forest. So, in the earlier scenes, the manifest presumption is that the pleasantly situated Glamis Castle would be a haven and a sanctuary, associated with temples by Macbeth as well as Banquo. Rapidly it proves to be the opposite for its guests, whereas those menacing thumps at the gateway announce the arrival not of a dangerous enemy but of their predestined ally. Despite his sacrifice and suffering, his quasi-miraculous birth, and his intervention on the side of the angels, I shall refrain from presenting Macduff as a Christ-figure. There are altogether too many of these in current literary criticism— many more, I fear, than exist in real life. Yet it is enlightening to consider the suggested analogy between this episode and that pageant in the mystery cycles which dramatizes the Harrowing of Hell. Some of those old guild-plays were still being acted during Shakespeare's boyhood; nearby Coventry was a center for them; and we meet with occasional allusions to them in Shakespeare's plays, notably to Herod whose furious ranting had made him a popular byword. Without the Slaughter of the Innocents, over which he presided, the horrendous slaughter at Macduff's castle would have been unthinkable. Many later audiences, which might have flinched, have been spared it.

When Jesus stands before the gates of hell, in the Wakefield cycle, his way is barred by a gatekeeper suggestively named Rybald, who tells his fellow devil Beelzebub to tie up those souls which are about to be delivered: "How, belsabub! bynde thise boys, / sich harow was never hard in hell." The command of Jesus that the gates he opened takes the form of a Latin cadence from the liturgy, *Attollite portas*. . . . This, in turn, is based upon the vulgate phrasing of the Twenty-fourth Psalm: "Lift up your heads, O ye gates; even lift them up, ye everlasting doors; and the King of glory shall come in." The liturgical Latin echoes the rite of Palm Sunday celebrating Christ's entrance into Jerusalem. It was also chanted before the portals of a church during the ceremonies of consecration. In the mystery, Jesus enters hell to debate with Satan and ends by rescuing therefrom various worthies out of the Old Testament. That is the typological situation which prefigured Shakespeare's comic gag. We must now turn back to his dilatory Porter, after having kept the visitor waiting outside longer than the Porter will. Obviously the action is continuous between scenes two and three, with the repeated knocking to mark the continuity. "Wake Duncan with thy knocking! I would thou couldst!" is the exit line (2.2.71). Macbeth, unnerved, is guided to their chamber by his wife, as he will be again in the Banquet Scene, and as she will imagine in the Sleepwalking Scene. There should be a minute when the stage is bare, and the only drama is the knocking.

But it will take a longer interval for the couple to wash off the blood and change into night attire. This is the theatrical necessity that provides the Porter with his cue and one of the troupe's comedians with a small part. Shakespeare's clowns tend to be more stylized than his other characters, most specifically the fools created by Robert Armin, and probably to reflect the personal style of certain actors. Will Kemp, who preceded Armin as principal comedian, seems to have specialized in voluble servants. It may well have been Kemp who created the rather similar roles of Launce in *The Two Gentlemen of Verona* and Launcelot Gobbo in *The Merchant of Venice*. Each of these has his characteristic routine: a monologue which becomes a dialogue as the speaker addresses himself to imagined interlocutors. Gobbo's is especially apropos, since it pits his conscience against the fiend. Shakespeare did not abandon that vein after Kemp left the company; indeed he brought it to its highest pitch of development in Falstaff's catechism on honor. The Porter's little act is pitched at a much lower level, yet it can be better understood in the light of such parallels. The sleepy Porter stumbles in, bearing the standard attributes of his office, a lantern and some keys. He is not drunk now; but, like others in the castle, he has been carousing late; and his fantasy may be inspired by the penitential mood of the morning after. "If a man were Porter of Hell Gate"—that is the hypothesis on which he is ready to act—"he should have old turning the key"— he should have to admit innumerable sinners (2.3.1–3).

An audience acquainted with Marlowe's *Doctor Faustus* would not have to be reminded that the hellmouth had figured in the mysteries. And the dramatist who had conceived the Brothel Scene in *Othello* had envisioned a character, namely Emilia, who could be accused of keeping—as the opposite number of Saint Peter—"the gate of hell" (4.2.92). The Porter assumes that stance by choice, asking himself: "Who's there, i' th' name of Belzebub?" (3–4). He answers himself by admitting three social offenders. It has been his plan, he then confides, to have passed in review "all professions," doubtless with an appropriately satirical comment on each (18). But, despite the histrionic pretence that hellfire is roaring away, the Porter's teeth are chattering in the chill of early morning: "this place is too cold for hell" (16–17). Neither the timeserving farmer nor the hose-stealing tailor seems as pertinent a wrongdoer as the equivocator, "who could not equivocate to heaven" (10–11). Here the editors digress to inform us about the trial and execution of Henry Garnet, Superior of the Jesuit Order, in 1606. The topical allusion is helpful, insofar as it indicates how the word came to be in the air; and Garnet's casuistry had to do with treason and attempted regicide, the notorious Gunpowder Plot. But *Macbeth* is not exactly a satire on the Jesuits. Maeterlinck, in his translation, renders "equivocator" by "*jésuite*" because there is no cognate French equivalent. The thematic significance of the Porter's speech lies in its anticipation of the oracles ("these juggling fiends"), which turn out to be true in an unanticipated sense: "th' equivocation of the fiend" (5.8.19; 5.5.42).

The Porter, who has been parrying the knocks by echoing them, finally shuffles to the gate, lets in Macduff and Lennox, and stands by for his tip: "I pray you remember the porter" (20–21). Drink, which has inebriated the grooms and emboldened Lady Macbeth, is his poor excuse for tardiness. The aftereffects of drinking are the subject of his vulgar and not very funny riddle: "nose-painting, sleep, and urine" (28). Then, licensed perhaps by the precedent of the devil-porter Rybald, he moves on to the equivocal subject of lechery. If drink provokes the desire but takes away the performance, it is a paradigm for Macbeth's ambition. For, as Lady Macbeth will realize: "Nought's had, all's spent, / Where our desire is got without content" (3.2.4–5). When the liquor is declared to be "an equivocator with lechery," that equivocation is demonstrated by the give-and-take of the Porter's rhythms: "it makes him, and it mars him; it sets him on, and it takes him off; it persuades him, and disheartens him; makes him stand to, and not stand to; in conclusion, equivocates him in a sleep, and giving him the lie, leaves him" (2.3.32–36). Each of these paired clauses, here again, links a false promise with a defeated expectation, expiring into drunken slumber after a moment of disappointed potency. The seesaw of the cadencing is as much of a prophecy as the Witches' couplets, and it has the advantage of pointing unequivocally toward the dénouement. The repartee trails off, after a lame pun about lying, with the reentrance of Macbeth, for which the Porter has been gaining time by going through his turn.

That turn has regularly been an object of expurgation, both in the theater and in print. I am not digressive if I recall that, when I wrote the introduction to a school-edition several years ago, the publishers wanted to leave out the Porter's ribaldry. I insisted upon an unbowdlerized text; but their apprehensions were commercially warranted; the textbook, though it is in a well-known series, has hardly circulated at all. Thousands of adolescents have been saved from the hazards of contemplating alcoholism, sex, and micturition. On a higher critical plane—some would say the highest—Coleridge was so nauseated by the whole scene that he ruled it out of the canon, declaring that it had been "written for the mob by another hand." The sentence about "the primrose way to th' everlasting bonfire," Coleridge conceded, had a Shakespearean ring (2.3.19). Without pausing to wonder whether it might have been echoed from *Hamlet,* he characteristically assumed that Shakespeare himself had interpolated it within the interpolation of his unknown collaborator. This enabled him to beg the question with Coleridgean logic and to comment further on "the entire absence of comedy, nay, even of irony . . . in *Macbeth.*" Wholly apart from the comedy or the authenticity of the Porter Scene, it must strike us as singularly obtuse to overlook the fundamental ironies of the play: its ambiguous predictions, its self-destructive misdeeds. It could be urged in Coleridge's defense, that the concept of dramatic irony had not yet been formulated. Kierkegaard's thesis on it was published in 1840, having been anticipated by Connop Thirlwall just a few years before.

Coleridge's rejection is sustained by another high literary authority. In Schiller's German adaptation, the Porter is high-minded and cold sober. He has stayed awake to keep guard over the King, and therefore over all Scotland, as he tells Macbeth in an ambitious jest. Instead of masquerading as an infernal gatekeeper, he has sung a pious hymn to the sunrise and has ignored the knocking in order to finish his *Morgenlied*. Yet, for a century now, the current of opinion has run the other way; commentators have held, with J. W. Hales, that Shakespeare's Porter was authentic and by no means inappropriate. Robert Browning heartily agreed, and Bishop Wordsworth even allowed that the scene could be read with edification. So it should be, given its eschatological overtones. We have long discarded the neoclassical inhibitions regarding the intermixture of tragic and comic elements. We have learned, above all from Lear's Fool, that the comic can intensify the tragic, rather than simply offer itself as relief. Those "secret, black, and midnight hags," the Witches, who for Holinshed were goddesses of destiny, come as close as anything in Shakespeare to the chorus of Greek tragedy (4.1.48). But their outlandish imminence seems elusive and amoral because of their mysterious connection with the machinery of fate. The Porter's role is grotesquely choric in another sense. Like the Gardener in *Richard II*, he stands there to point the moral, to act out the object-lesson. This castle, far from reaching up toward heaven, is located at the brink of hell. Even now its lord has damned himself eternally.

Damnation is portended by the curse of sleeplessness, which has been foreshadowed among the spells that the First Witch proposed to cast upon the seacaptain: "Sleep shall neither night nor day / Hang upon his penthouse lid" (1.3.19–20). No sooner has the King been murdered than Macbeth hears the voice crying "Sleep no more!" and begins to extoll the blessing he has forfeited. The word itself is sounded thirty-two times, more than in any other play of Shakespeare's. Repeatedly sleep is compared with death. Almost enviously, after complaining of the "terrible dreams" that afflict him nightly, Macbeth evokes the buried Duncan: "After life's fitful fever he sleeps well" (3.2.18, 23). When he breaks down at the Banquet Scene before the apparition of Banquo's ghost, it is Lady Macbeth who assumes command, discharges the guests, and leads her husband off to bed with the soothing words: "You lack the season of all natures, sleep" (3.4.140). It should be noted that she does not see the ghost or hear the voice, and that she skeptically dismisses the air-drawn dagger as a subjective phenomenon: "the very painting of your fear" (3.4.60). Unlike Macbeth, she has no intercourse with the supernatural forces. To be sure, she has called upon the spirits to unsex her, fearing lest she be deterred from murder by the milk— the feminine attribute—of human kindness. And from the outset it is he, not she, who feels and expresses that remorse she has steeled herself against, those "compunctious visitings of nature" (1.5.45). When they ultimately overtake her, his insomnia will have its counterpart in her somnambulism.

In keeping with her aloofness from supernaturalism, Shakespeare's treatment of her affliction seems so naturalistic that it is now and then cited among the clinical cases in abnormal psychology. According to the seventeenth-century frame of reference, she may show the symptoms of melancholia or—to invoke theological concepts that still can grip the audiences of films—demonic possession. Psychoanalysis tends to diagnose her malady as a manifestation of hysteria, which compels her to dramatize her anxiety instead of dreaming about it, to reenact the pattern of behavior that she has tried so desperately to repress. Freud regarded this sleepwalker and her sleepless mate as "two disunited parts of a single psychical individuality," together subsuming the possibilities of reaction to the crime, and underlined the transference from his response to hers, from his hallucinations to her mental disorder. In more social terms, the closeness of their complementary relationship seems strongly reinforced by the sexual bond between them. Three of the exit-lines emphasize their going to bed together. Caroline Spurgeon and other interpreters of Shakespeare's imagery have noticed that the most recurrent metaphor in the play has to do with dressing and undressing, transposed sometimes into arming and disarming or crowning and uncrowning. The sense of intimacy is enhanced by the recollection that the nightgowns mentioned are dressing gowns, that under the bedclothes no clothing of any sort was worn in that day; and nakedness exposed is one of the other themes (a recent film has welcomed the opportunity for presenting a heroine in the nude). Lady Macbeth, as M. C. Bradbrook has observed, must have been a siren as well as a fury.

Inquiries into her motives have dwelt upon her childlessness, after having borne a child who evidently died, and that frustration seems to have kindled Macbeth's hostility toward the families of Banquo and Macduff. Deprived of happy motherhood, she takes a somewhat maternal attitude toward her spouse, and she seeks a vicarious fulfillment in her ruthless ambitions for his career. Holinshed had stressed her single-minded goading-on of her husband, "burning in unquenchable desire to bear the name of a queen." She may be a "fiend-like queen" to Malcolm and other enemies, but the characterization is highly nuanced when we contrast it with the termagant queens of Shakespeare's earliest histories (5.9.35). Criticism ranges all the way from Hazlitt ("a great bad woman whom we hate, but whom we fear more than we hate") to Coleridge ("a woman of a visionary and daydreaming turn of mind"). Coleridge had re-created Hamlet in his own image, after all, and his Lady Macbeth might pose as a model for Madame Bovary. The variance in interpretations extends from Lamartine's "perverted and passionate woman" to Tieck's emphasis on her conjugal tenderness, which provoked the mockery of Heine, who envisages her billing and cooing like a turtle dove. She may not be "such a dear" as Bernard Shaw discerned in Ellen Terry's portrayal; but she encompasses most of these images, inasmuch as Shakespeare clearly understood the ambivalence of aggression and sympathy in human beings. Her emotions and Macbeth's are timed to a different rhythm. As he hardens into a fighting posture, and his innate virility reasserts itself, she softens into fragile femininity, and her insecurities come to the surface of her breakdown.

Distraction of the mind is rendered by Shakespeare in a pithy, terse, staccato idiom which might not inappropriately be termed distracted prose. Madness, along with all the other moods of English tragedy, had originally been conveyed through blank verse, as when Titus Andronicus "runs lunatic." So it was in Kyd's operatic *Spanish Tragedy,* though the later and more sophisticated ragings of its hero would be added by another hand in prose. The innovation was Marlowe's: in the first part of *Tamburlaine* the captive queen Zabina goes mad over the death of her consort Bajazet, and before her suicide gives utterance to a short prose sequence of broken thoughts. Her farewell line, "Make ready my coach," must have given Shakespeare a suggestion for Ophelia. He seized upon this technique and developed it to the point where it became, in the phrase of Laertes, "A document in madness, / Thoughts and remembrance fitted." Ophelia distributing flowers, like King Lear distributing weeds, obsessively renews the source of grief. Edgar in the guise of Tom o' Bedlam deliberately imitates such language as does Hamlet when he simulates insanity. Lear's Fool is exceptional, since he is both a jester and a natural; yet, in that dual role, he may be looked upon as a mediator between the comic and the distracted prose. And in *King Lear* as a whole, in the interrelationship between the Lear-Cordelia plot and the Gloucester-Edgar underplot, we have our most highly wrought example of the two plots running parallel. As a matter of dramaturgic tradition, that parallel tended in the direction of parody.

Thus, in the Second Shepherds' Play at Wakefield, the serious plot about the nativity is parodied by the sheepstealing underplot, since the lamb is an emblem of Jesus. In the oldest English secular comedy, *Fulgens and Lucres,* while two suitors court the mistress, their respective servants court the maid—probably the most traditional of all comic situations, harking back as far as Aristophanes' *Frogs.* In *Doctor Faustus* the clowns burlesque the hero's conjurations by purloining his magical book and conjuring up a demon. This has its analogue in *The Tempest,* where the conspiracy against Prospero is burlesqued by the clownish complot. Having defended the essential seriousness of the Porter's Scene, I am not moving toward an argument that there is anything comic per se in the Sleepwalking Scene; but there is something distinctly parodic about the virtual repetition of a previous scene in such foreshortened and denatured form. Murder will out, as the old adage cautions; the modern detective story operates on the assumption that the murderer returns to the locality of the crime. Lady Macbeth, always brave and bold when her husband was present, must sleep alone when he departs for the battlefield. It is then that her suppressed compunction, her latent sense of guilt, wells up from the depths of her subconscious anguish. Under the cover of darkness and semi-consciousness, she must now reenact her part, going through the motions of that scene in the courtyard on the night of Duncan's assassination, and recapitulating the crucial stages of the entire experience.

When the late Tyrone Guthrie staged his production at the Old Vic, he directed his leading lady, Flora Robson, to reproduce the exact gesticulation of the murder scene. Such an effect could not have been achieved within the Piranesilike setting designed by Gordon Craig, where the sleepwalking was supposed to take place on the steps of a sweeping spiral staircase. One of the most theatrical features of this episode, however it be played, lies in the choreographic opportunity that it offers to the actress and the director. At the Globe Playhouse the principal problem in staging would have been the glaring fact that plays were performed there in broad daylight. That was simply met by a convention, which has been uncovered through the researches of W. J. Laurence. A special point was made of bringing out lanterns, tapers, or other lights, paradoxically enough, to indicate the darkness. But the lighting of the Sleepwalking Scene is not merely conventional. Lady Macbeth, we learn, can no longer abide the dark. "She has light by her continually," her Waiting Gentlewoman confides to the Doctor (5.1.22–23). It is the candle she carries when she enters, no mere stage property either, throwing its beams like a good deed in a naughty world. Banquo, on a starless night, has referred metaphorically to the overclouded stars as extinguished candles. Macbeth, when the news of his wife's suicide is subsequently brought to him, will inveigh against the autumnal prospect of meaninglessness ahead, and the yesterdays behind that have "lighted fools / The way to dusty death" (5.5.22–23). Life itself is the brief candle he would now blow out.

Lady Macbeth presumably carried her candle throughout the scene until the London appearance of Sarah Siddons in 1785. She was severely criticized for setting it down on a table, so that she could pantomime the gesture of rubbing her hands. Sheridan, then manager of the Drury Lane, told her: "It would be thought a presumptuous innovation." Man of the theater that he was, he congratulated her upon it afterwards. But many in the audience were put off by it, and even more by her costume. She was wearing white satin, traditionally reserved for mad scenes, and later on would shift to a shroud-like garment. Mrs. Siddons as Lady Macbeth became, by wide consent, the greatest English actress in her greatest role. Hence we have a fair amount of testimony about her performance. A statuesque figure whose rich voice ranged from melancholy to peevishness, subsiding at times into eager whispers, she was "tragedy personified" for Hazlitt, who reports that "all her gestures were involuntary and mechanical." More physically active than her candle-burdened predecessors, who seem to have mainly glided, she excelled particularly at stagebusiness. The hand-rubbing was accompanied by a gesture of ladling water out of an imaginary ewer. When she held up one hand, she made a face at the smell—a bit of business which Leigh Hunt considered "unrefined." Yet, after she had made her exit stalking backwards, one witness testified: "I swear that I smelt blood!" She herself has attested that, when as a girl of twenty she began to study the part, she was overcome by a paroxysm of terror.

Turning more directly to "this slumb'ry agitation," we are pre-

pared for it by the expository conversation between the Gentlewoman and the Doctor (5.1.11). Lady Macbeth's twenty lines will
be punctuated by their whispering comments. It is clear that there
have been earlier visitations, and that Lady Macbeth has engaged in
writing during one of them; but what she spoke the Gentlewoman
firmly refuses to disclose. The Doctor, who has been watching with
her during the last two nights, has so far witnessed nothing. But,
from the account, he knows what to expect: "A great perturbation
in nature, to receive at once the benefit of sleep and do the effects of
watching!" (9–11). Sleep seems scarcely a benefit under the circumstances, much as it may be longed for by the watchful, the ever-
wakeful Macbeth; and, though Lady Macbeth is actually sleeping,
she is not only reliving the guilty past but incriminating herself.
When she appears, the antiphonal comment ("You see her eyes are
open." / "Ay, but their sense is shut.") raises that same question of
moral blindness which Shakespeare explored in *King Lear* (24–25).
If she could feel that her hands were cleansed when she washed them,
her compulsive gesture would be a ritual of purification. Yet Pilate,
washing his hands before the multitude, has become an archetype of
complicity. Her opening observation and exclamation ("Yet here's a
spot" . . . "Out, damn'd spot!") is a confession that prolonged and
repeated ablutions have failed to purge her sins (31, 35). She continues by imagining that she hears the clock strike two: it is time
for the assassination. Her revulsion from it compresses into three
words all the onus of the Porter's garrulous commentary: "Hell is
murky" (36).

That sudden glimpse of the bottomless pit does not keep her
from the sanguinary course she has been pursuing. But the grandiose
iambic pentameter of her courtyard speeches, inspiriting and rebuk-
ing her reluctant partner, has been contracted into a spasmodic series
of curt, stark interjections, most of them monosyllabic. "Yet who
would have thought the old man to have had so much blood in him?"
(39–40). She had thought at least of her father, and had momentarily
recoiled. Macbeth had feared that the deed might not "trammel up
the consequence," might open the way for retributive counteraction,
and indeed Duncan's blood has clamored for a terrible augmentation
of bloodshed, has set off the chain reaction of blood feuds involving
Banquo's progeny and Macduff's. Hitherto we had not been aware
of Lady Macbeth's awareness of the latter, much less of how she
might respond to his catastrophe. Her allusion to Lady Macduff

seems reduced to the miniature scale of a nursery rhyme ("The Thane of Fife / had a wife"), but it culminates in the universal lamentation of *ubi est:* "Where is she now?" Then, more hand-washing, more conjugal reproach. Her listeners are realizing, more and more painfully, that they should not be listening; what she says should not be heard, should not have been spoken, should never have happened. "Here's the smell of the blood still" (50). The olfactory metaphor has a scriptural sanction, as Leigh Hunt should have remembered: evil was a stench in righteous nostrils, and the offence of Claudius smelled to heaven. The heartcry comes with the recognition that the smell of blood will be there forever: "All the perfumes of Arabia will not sweeten this little hand" (50–51).

She had been clear headed, tough-minded, and matter-of-fact in tidying up after the murder: "A little water clears us of this deed." It was Macbeth, exhausted and conscience-stricken after his monstrous exertion, who had envisioned its ethical consequences in a hyperbolic comparison:

> Will all great Neptune's ocean wash this blood
> Clean from my hand? No; this my hand will rather
> The multitudinous seas incarnadine,
> Making the green one red.
>
> (2.2.57–60)

Her hand is smaller than his, and so—relatively speaking—is her hyperbole. All the perfumes of Arabia, all the oil wells of Arabia, could not begin to fill the amplitude of the ocean, and the contrast is completed by the oceanic swell of his Latinate polysyllables. She has come to perceive, unwillingly and belatedly, that the stigmata are irremovable. He had perceived this at once and, moreover, reversed his magniloquent trope. Never can the bloodstain be cleansed away; on the contrary, it will pollute the world. No one can, as she advised in another context, "lave our honors" (3.2.33). The sound that voices this perception on her part ("O, O, O!") was more than a sign when Mrs. Siddons voiced it, we are told (5.1.52). It was "a convulsive shudder—very horrible." The one-sided marital dialogue goes on, reverting to the tone of matter-of-factness. "Wash your hands, put on your nightgown, look not so pale" (62–63). If Duncan is in his grave, as Macbeth has mused, is not Banquo in a similar condition? Where is he now? Reminiscence here reverberates from the Banquet Scene: "I tell you yet again, Banquo's buried; he cannot come out on's grave" (63–64). These internalized anxieties that will not be so coolly exorcized are far more harrowing than the externalized ghosts that beset Richard III on the eve of battle. Having resumed his soldierly occupation and been reassured by the Witches' auguries, Macbeth has put fear behind him, whatever the other cares that are crowding upon him. It is therefore through Lady Macbeth that we apprehend the approach of nemesis.

And then her terminal speech: "To bed, to bed; there's knocking at the gate" (66–67). It is imaginary knocking; what we hear again is silence, a silence powerful enough to resurrect the encounter between those harbingers of revenge and damnation, Macduff and the Porter. Her fantasy concludes by repeating what we have already watched in both the Murder Scene and the Banquet Scene, when she led her faltering husband offstage. "Come, come, come, come, give me your hand" (67). Her next and penultimate remark harks back to the concatenation of earlier events. The First Witch, in her premonitory resentment against the sailor's wife, had promised him a swarm of nameless mischiefs (future tense): "I'll do, I'll do, and I'll do" (1.3.10). Macbeth's own ruminations at the edge of action had started from the premise (present tense, conditional and indicative): "If it were done, when 'tis done, then 'twere well / It were done quickly" (1.7.1–2). It was done quickly, whereupon Lady Macbeth sought to arrest his mounting disquietude with the flat affirmation (past, transitive): "What's done, is done" (3.2.12). Similar as it sounds, it was a far cry from her concluding negation, here fatalistic valediction to life: "What's done cannot be undone" (5.1.68). This implies the wish that it had not been done, reinforces Macbeth's initial feeling that it need not be done, and equilibrates the play's dialectical movement between free will and inevitability. The appeal, "To bed," is uttered five times. She moves off to the bedchamber they will never share again, as if she still were guiding her absent husband's steps and his bloodstained hand were still in hers.

The doctor, who has been taking notes, confesses himself to be baffled. The case is beyond his practise, it requires a divine rather than a physician. In the following scene he discusses it with Macbeth on a more or less psychiatric basis. Lady Macbeth is "Not so sick . . . / As she is troubled with thick-coming fancies, / That keep her from her rest" (5.3.37–39). The Doctor is not a psychiatrist; he cannot "minister to a mind disease'd" (40). Nor has he a cure for Scotland's disease, when Macbeth rhetorically questions him. Here we catch the connection with the one scene that passes in England, where the dramatic values center on Macduff's reaction to his domestic tragedy. His interview with Malcolm is a test of loyalty, and the invented accusations that Malcolm levels against himself—that he would, for instance, "Pour the sweet milk of concord into hell"—are more applicable to Macbeth, whose milky nature has gone just that way (4.3.98). We are at the court of Edward the Confessor, the saintly English king whose virtues make him a foil for the Scottish hellhound. A passage which might seem to be a digression expatiates on how the royal touch can cure his ailing subjects of the scrofula, known accordingly as the King's Evil. Shakespeare is complimenting the new Stuart monarch, James I, descendant of the legendary Banquo, who had revived the ancient superstition. But the pertinence goes further; for the spokesman of the English king is another doctor; and the antithesis is brought home when we compare the sickness of the one country with that of the other. The King's Evil? Given the omens, the tidings, the disaffections, is it not Scotland which suffers from that disease?

A. C. Bradley asserted that Lady Macbeth is "the only one of Shakespeare's great tragic characters who on a last appearance is denied the dignity of verse." That comment discloses a curious insensitivity not only to the ways of the theater, which never interested Bradley very much, but to the insights of psychology, for which he claimed an especial concern. It could be maintained that distracted prose constitutes an intensive vein of poetry. Somnambulism, though fairly rare as a habit among adults (much rarer than sleep-talking), is such a striking one that we might expect it to have had more impact upon the imagination. Yet there seems to be little or no folklore about it, if we may judge from its omission in Stith Thompson's comprehensive *Index*. It has suggested that the rather silly libretto of Bellini's opera, *La Sonnambula* (based upon a vaudeville-ballet by Scribe), where the sleepwalking heroine compromises herself by walking into a man's room at an inn, and then redeems her reputation by singing a coloratura aria while perambulating asleep on a rooftop. Dissimilarly, Verdi's *Macbetto* avoids such pyrotechnical possibilities. The prima donna, in her sleepwalking *scena,* sticks fairly close to Shakespeare's disjointed interjections, though her voice mounts to a Verdian lilt at the high point:

> Arabia intera
> rimandar sí piccol mano
> co' suoi balsami non puó,
> no, no, non puó.

The only serious dramatization that I can recall, apart from Shakespeare's, is Kleist's *Prinz Friedrich von Homburg*. In contradistinction to Lady Macbeth, Prince Friedrich has already made his promenade when the play opens; he is discovered at morning seated in a garden; and the garland he is unconsciously weaving adumbrates his dreams of future military glory. The title of Hermann Broch's fictional trilogy, *Die Schlafwandler,* is purely figurative. A melodrama made famous by Henry Irving, *The Bells,* culminates in the mesmerized reenactment of a crime. It is worth noting that the first *Macbeth* acted in German (1773), freely adapted by Gottlob Stefanie der Jüngere, replaced the sleepwalking scene by a mad scene in which Macbeth was stabbed to death by his lady. Shakespeare would seem to have been as unique in his choice of subject as in his handling of it.

There is nothing to prevent a mad scene from taking place in the daytime. But Lady Macbeth must be a noctambulist as well as a somnambulist, for her climactic episode brings out the nocturnal shading of the tragedy. *Macbeth,* from first to last, is deeply and darkly involved with the nightside of things. Both Macbeth and Lady Macbeth apostrophize the darkness, calling upon it to cover their malefactions. The timing of crucial scenes is conveyed, not merely by the convention of lighting candles, but by the recurring imagery of nightfall, overcast and dreamlike as in the dagger speech:

> Now o'er the one half world
> Nature seems dead, and wicked dreams abuse
> The curtain'd sleep.
>
> (2.1.49–51)

Characters, habitually undressing or dressing, seem to be either going to bed or getting up, like the Porter when he is so loudly wakened. "Light thickens," and the mood can be summed up by the protagonist in a single couplet:

> Good things of day begin to droop and drowse,
> Whiles night's black agents to their preys do rouse.
>
> (3.2.52–53)

Critical decisions are reached and fell designs are carried out at hours when night is "Almost at odds with morning, which is which," when the atmosphere—like hell—is murky, and it is hard to distinguish fair from foul or foul from fair (3.4.126). The penalty for wilfulness is watchfulness, in the sense of staying awake against one's will, of fitfully tossing and turning between bad dreams. Existence has become a watching, a waking, a walking dream. Yet "night's predominance," as one of the Thanes describes it, cannot last forever (2.4.8). Malcolm offers consolation by saying: "The night is long that never finds the day" (4.3.240). Macduff is fated to bring in the head of Macbeth on a pike, like the Thane of Cawdor's at the beginning, and to announce the good word: "the time is free" (5.9.21). The human makes its reflux over the fiendish at long last. After so painful and protracted an agony, after a spell so oneiric and so insomniac by turns, we welcome the daylight as if we were awakening from a nightmare.

# "Thriftless Ambition," Foolish Wishes, and the Tragedy of *Macbeth*

*Robert N. Watson*

The crude outlines of *Macbeth* as a moral drama are visible in Elizabethan panegyrics to universal order:

> Now if nature should intermit her course, and leave altogether though it were but for a while the observation of her own laws . . . if the prince of the lights of heaven, which now as a giant doth run his unwearied course, should as it were through a languishing faintness begin to stand and to rest himself; if . . . the times and seasons of the year [should] blend themselves by disordered and confused mixture . . . the fruits of the earth pine away as children at the withered breasts of their mother no longer able to yield them relief: what would become of man himself, whom these things now do all serve?

A dozen years after Hooker's "Laws of Ecclesiastical Polity" asked these questions, Shakespeare's *Macbeth* provided some fairly conventional answers: man himself becomes a disordered mixture, with no regenerative cycles to rescue him from his mortality and no social system to deliver him from his evil impulses. The cosmic and bodily disorders that accompany Macbeth's rebellion distinctly resemble the ones predicted in the official "Exhortation Concerning Good Order, and Obedience to Rulers and Magistrates":

From *Shakespeare and the Hazards of Ambition.* © 1984 by the President and Fellows of Harvard College. Harvard University Press, 1984.

> The earth, trees, seeds, plants . . . keep themselves in their order: all the parts of the whole year, as winter, summer, months, nights, and days, continue in their order . . . and man himself also hath all his parts both within and without, as soul, heart, mind, memory, understanding, reason, speech, with all and singular corporal members of his body, in a profitable, necessary, and pleasant order: every degree of people . . . hath appointed to them their duty and order: some are in high degree, some in low, some kings and princes, some inferiors and subjects . . . and every one hath need of other . . . Take away kings, princes . . . and such estates of God's order, no man shall ride or go by the highway unrobbed, no man shall sleep in his own house or bed unkilled, no man shall keep his wife, children, and possessions in quietness . . . and there must needs follow all mischief and utter destruction both of souls, bodies, goods, and commonwealths.

In *Macbeth* as in *Richard III,* this deadly loss of personal and natural integrity does not result (as in Hooker) from some careless indolence of the world's ordering forces, but rather (as in the "Exhortation") from a human determination to disturb the political aspect of that order. In murdering the princes who would exclude him from the throne, Richard willingly "smothered / The most replenished sweet work of Nature / That from the prime creation e'er she fram'd" (4.3.17–19). In unseating Duncan, Macbeth willingly made "a breach in nature" through which "the wine of life" was drained (2.3.113, 95). Both usurpers push back toward primal chaos a Creation that thwarts their desires, hoping to reconstruct it in the image and likeness of their aspiring minds. Ambition, in its inherent opposition to heredity and the established order, thus becomes the enemy of all life, especially that of the ambitious man himself.

But these passages, like most others cited by critics seeking to define a unified "Elizabethan world view," are taken from works expressly written in defense of England's political and theological authorities. Those authorities had a tremendous stake in maintaining order and hierarchy, and in defining them as natural and divinely ordained. If we can recognize in such passages the voice of self-serving pragmatism rather than objective philosophy, we can infer a contrary voice, the voice of the disempowered that the propaganda is struggling to refute. To understand Shakespeare's play, as to understand English cultural history as a whole, requires this sort of inference. The play, like history, like the witches who are agents of them both, "palter[s] with us in a double sense" (5.8.20). Where the witches' prophecies seem to endorse ambition, but warn on a more literal and less audible level against its futility, *Macbeth* contains a silent, figurative endorsement of ambition, even while loudly and eloquently restating the principles expressed by Hooker and the "Exhortation Concerning Good Order."

The spirit of tragedy itself cuts against such single-minded, heavy-handed moralizations, striving subversively on behalf of the individual human will. Shakespeare moves from history to tragedy by clarifying and universalizing the hazards of ambition: this cautionary pattern, which was shaped by the propagandistic aspect of *Richard III,* creates its own sort of moral drama in *Macbeth.* We may view Richard with horrified admiration, but we identify with Macbeth from within. Shakespeare accomplishes this, makes Macbeth eligible for the fear and pity that permit catharsis, by encoding many of our repressed impulses, many of the rash wishes society has obliged us to abandon or conceal, within Macbeth's conventionally dramatic desire to replace the king. In his soliloquy before the regicide, Macbeth acknowledges that his deed will entail all the kinds of violence civilization has been struggling to suppress since it first began: violence between the guest and the host, violence by subjects against a monarch, and violence among kinspeople. When Shakespeare wants to show society's descent into utter deprivacy in *King Lear,* the moral holocaust consists of exactly these crimes: crimes against the host Gloucester, crimes against the royal father Lear, and crimes among siblings over legacies and lovers. In fact, Macbeth's misdeed resembles the one Freud says civilization was formed to suppress: the murder of the ruling father of the first human clan because he refused to share his reproductive privileges with his filial subjects.

In the history plays, Shakespeare established Oedipal desires as a metaphor for ambition; in *Macbeth,* he exploits the metaphor to implicate his audience in the ambitious crime, by tapping its guilt-ridden urges against authority and even against reality. On an individual as well as a racial scale, the Oedipal patterns psychoanalytic critics have noticed in this play, with Duncan as a father-figure and Lady Macbeth as the sinister temptress who is both mother and wife, may be a way of making the men in the audience intuitively identify with Macbeth's wish fulfillment. For most young men, that Oedipal guilt is a perfect focal point for more general resentments like the ones that turn Macbeth against Duncan: resentments against those who have power over us, those who have things we want, and those whom we want to become. The conflicts Shakespeare is addressing here are not merely the sexual ones. As he demonstrates the deeper meanings and broader ramifications of ambition, he necessarily implies that any desire to change the given order is a scion of that sin; and such a moral inevitably collides with the basic imperatives of life. To live is to change the world, to shape the environment to meet one's needs; even before the Oedipal phase begins, every infant is profoundly involved in a struggle to learn how far that shaping can go, and how best to perform it. So what might at first have been merely analogies or resonances by which Shakespeare suggested the foundations of his cautionary political tales become, in *Macbeth,* the openings through which we enter the story and receive the tragic experience.

To make these openings more accessible, Shakespeare expands and details a motif implicit in the history plays' treatment of ambition: the "foolish wish" motif of folklore, in which a person's unenlightened way of desiring converts the power of gaining desires into a curse. Richard III and Henry IV pursue an unlineal, unnatural kingship, and that is precisely what they get, much to their distress. In *Macbeth* this motif acquires the imaginative breadth, and hence the universal applicability, that it has in fairy tales, where it usually involves a narrow-minded disruption of nature's complex balances. The stories achieve their cautionary effect by showing the logical but terrifying ramifications of having such wishes granted. King Midas, for example, acquires the golden touch only to discover that it isolates him from food, love, and family—all the joys of natural life. Perhaps more strikingly relevant to *Macbeth* is the Grimm Brothers' story called "The Fisherman and His Wife." The humble man discovers a magic fish in his net and, at the insistence of his shrewish wife, obliges it to replace their hovel with a castle. The wife steadily increases her demands for splendor and power, the ocean becomes angrier with each new request, and the couple becomes more discontented after each wish is granted, until the fish finally returns them to their original humble state.

But once Macbeth has rashly "done the deed" of self-promotion at his wife's instigation, they both learn that "What's done cannot be undone" (2.2.14; 5.1.68). Bruno Bettelheim "cannot recall a single fairy tale in which a child's angry wishes have any [irreversible] consequence; only those of adults do. The implication is that adults are accountable for what they do." As such tales fascinate children by providing them with metaphorically coded lessons about the conduct of their own, more basic problems, so *Macbeth* conveys its harsher lessons to us. We do not need magic fish or bloodthirsty witches to provoke us; nature doth teach us all to have aspiring minds, as Tamburlaine asserts, or at least fickle and envious minds. We desire this man's art and that man's scope, with what we most enjoy contented least. Shakespeare alerts us to the fact that, to this extent, we participate in the murderous ambition we witness on stage, creating and suffering its poetically just consequences. While the official homilies claim that rebellion contains all other sins and provokes universal alterations, *Macbeth* suggests reciprocally that all other sins—indeed, all impulses toward change—partake of rebellion.

Foolish-wish stories serve to develop in the child a mechanism and a rationale of repression, a necessary device for subordinating immediate urges to long-term goals and abstract rules—necessary, because infantile desires are no less selfish, violent, and murkily incestuous than the ones propelling Macbeth. Human beings seem to share a stock of foolish wishes, and society survives on its ability to discourage their fulfillment. That may be one reason why the play (as several of its directors have emphasized) suggests that this crisis is only one instance of an endless cycle of rebellion: the play is less the story of two evil people than it is a representation of impulses—ambitious, rebellious, Oedipal—that the hierarchical structures of family and society arouse in every human life. Normal behavior resembles Macbeth's successful curbing of insurrection's lavish spirit early in the play; but deeply human motives constantly impel each person toward a comparable rebellion, differing in scale but not necessarily in basic character from Macbeth's.

In opposing the lineal succession to Scotland's throne, Macbeth and his wife foolishly wish regenerative nature out of existence, then suffer the consequences of their wishes' fulfillment. An attack on the cycle of parents and children necessarily affronts the cycles of night and day, sleeping and waking, and planting and harvesting, as well. Perhaps Rosse's warning against "Thriftless ambition, that will ravin up / Thine own live's means (2.4.28–29) seems all too obvious a moral, but it is worth remembering that Rosse here supposes that his observation refers simply to a patricide; the play obliges us to generalize it for him, into an axiom about our relationship to great creating nature as a whole. Even this grander lesson, that people should not rashly disrupt the web of nature for the sake of their individual desires, was as clearly deducible from the Elizabethan concept of a beneficent universe as from the modern concept of ecological networks. Some seventy-five years earlier, John Heywood's "Play of the Wether" ridiculed the idea of tampering with that natural system to satisfy the whims of individuals. There needs no ghost come on the stage to tell us this.

But evidently it was not obvious enough for Macbeth and Lady Macbeth, and in a sense it is not obvious enough for anyone who has ever idly wished for more light in December, more flowers in February, or less rain in April. In a fairy tale such wishes would cost us dearly, and justly; yet we cannot really feel guilty for having them. In his susceptibility to conventional human desires, and his momentary willingness to forget the reasons they must be suppressed, Macbeth is one of us. He shows us the logical extension, and the logical costs, of our own frailties. Macbeth merely encounters those frailties in a situation that magnifies them into something momentous and horrible; and he encounters them in a dramatic context that blurs the borderline between nightmarish fantasy and reality. When the witches first appear, they take us into a region where the distinction becomes foggy; when they first appear to Macbeth, they do the same for him. Their status as partly a product of his mind and partly actual witches, and their talent for self-fulfilling prophecy, confirm that liminal function. They convey him, as they convey us, into a world where one might suddenly find one's destructive impulses magically fulfilled, where crimes are "thought and done" simultaneously (4.1.149). Place any person in such a world, and who should 'scape whipping, or even hanging for murder; though we are indifferent honest, we could accuse us of such things that it were better our mothers had not borne us. If we can recognize Macbeth's crime as essentially an extension of our most casual recalcitrance at the ways of natural and social order, a symbolic performance of our resentful impulses against the aspects of the world that inconvenience us, we may find it hard to hold him accountable for his sin. The Porter and Macbeth have much to say against equivocators in this play (2.3.8–

36; 5.5.42), but Shakespeare himself performs a Jesuitical equivocation in conveying the play's beliefs. Everything on the play's stated level follows the orthodox line against ambition; the heresy resides where the words trail off into unspoken thoughts, Shakespeare's and ours, a heresy that (to state the case most extremely) portrays Macbeth as a martyr who dies for our sins at the hands of an order so strictly repressive that it makes the very business of living a punishable crime.

## THE VENGEANCE OF REGENERATIVE NATURE

The foolish-wife motif, with its overtones of poetic justice, was extremely popular among Jacobean moralists, particularly those warning young men against defying their fathers' instructions and leaving their hereditary places. Samuel Gardiner's *Portraiture of the Prodigal Sonne* declares that "there is nothing that hurteth so much as the having of our wils," and elsewhere that "a sinner may be killed with his owne poyson, even the poyson of his sinne"; several other prodigal-son tracts echo this idea. Macbeth himself worries about teaching

> Bloody instructions, which, being taught, return
> To plague th' inventor. This even-handed justice
> Commends th' ingredient of our poison'd chalice
> To our own lips.
>
> (1.7.7–12)

We can see, even if Macbeth cannot, how this axiom about regicide applies to the violations of universal order implied in that regicide, just as we could see that Rosse's remark about "thriftless ambition" could apply to any assault on sovereign nature as well as to a patricide. Henry IV's practical fear of counterusurpation thus expands into a tragic intuition about Pyrrhic victories over regenerative nature.

Macbeth and his Lady find their entire world sickened by the poisonous gall they fed to the Scottish body politic in place of its nurturant milk. Like Richard Brathwait's prodigal-son figure, Macbeth is "ill to others, worst unto himselfe." He murders sleep and plunges the world into an uneasy darkness, but he and his wife suffer the worst insomnia of all, and the long night exhausts them before finding day in Malcolm's vengeful return. They attempt to steal life and patrimony from the new generation of babes, but die without a living heir. The kingdom's vegetation, like its sunlight, fades at Duncan's death, but while Macbeth's life falls "into the sear, the yellow leaf" (5.3.23), Malcolm echoes his father's metaphors of seeds and planting in reclaiming his father's throne. In a stratagem that resembles a Maying festival, Birnam Wood comes like a sudden spring to the walls of Dunsinane castle. Sun, sons, and seedlings all return together to destroy the man whose ambition has made him their enemy.

The fisherman's wife in the Grimm Brothers' story crossed into the realm of the forbidden when she demanded control over the sun and the moon; Lady Macbeth provokes and performs a similar ambitious violation. When she exults that the regicide "shall to all our nights and days to come / Give solely sovereign sway and masterdom" (1.5.69–70), we may detect an aspiration to sovereignty *over* those nights and days, as well as during them. Bettelheim observes that "Many fairy tales depict the tragic outcome of . . . rash wishes, engaged in because one desires something too much or is unable to wait until things come about in their good time." As long as Macbeth plans to let natural events gain him the throne, he thinks in terms of letting time run its diurnal course. His aside about letting chance "crown me without my stir" is immediately followed by his aside that "Come what come may, / Time and the hour run through the roughest day" (1.3.144–48). But when Duncan extends that cyclical inevitability to include the succession of son as well as sun, Macbeth attacks the balance of light and dark as well as the unity of his own identity in opposing Duncan's choice: "Stars, hide your fires, / Let not light see my black and deep desires; / The eye wink at the hand" (1.4.50–52).

In the following scene, Lady Macbeth suggests a similar pair of assaults, against light and organic identity, to aid the assault on Duncan. Her first words are read from her husband's letter about the witches: "They met me in the day of success" (1.5.1). But the witches specialize in false encouragement and secondary meanings: daylight and succession are precisely what they induce this couple to sacrifice. Lady Macbeth quickly concludes that she must eradicate the vision daylight permits, along with the nursing succession demands, in order to fulfill the witches' promise:

> Come to my woman's breasts,
> And take my milk for gall, you murth'ring ministers,

> Wherever in your sightless substances
> You wait on nature's mischief! Come, thick night,
> And pall thee in the dunnest smoke of hell,
> That my keen knife see not the wound it makes,
> Nor heaven peep through the blanket of the dark
> To cry, "Hold, hold!"
>
> (1.5.47–54)

She will abandon her maternal role in the nursery in favor of a phallic role in the bedroom. To engineer their rebirths as monarchs, she and her husband will perform a forbidden deed on the paternal Duncan, under a blanket that leaves us uncertain whether the deed is essentially sexual or essentially violent. Such a cover is useful, not only in preventing Macbeth from thinking conscientiously of his mother and Lady Macbeth of her father (1.5.16–18; 2.2.12–13), but also in making us think about Shakespeare's symbolic pattern, which blends incest with parricide, and insemination with Caesarean section, in the forbidden act of self-remaking.

These requests for a crime-facilitating darkness soon lead to inadvertent predictions that the crime will actually forestall the progress of night into day. As they test each other's susceptibility to the idea of regicide, Lady Macbeth asks when Duncan will leave their castle. When Macbeth answers, "To-morrow, as he purposes," she exclaims, "O, never / Shall sun that morrow see!" (1.5.59–61). She means that Duncan will not live to go forth—*that* day will never come, we might say—but by saying it indirectly, she seems to imply that the murder will deprive future days of sunlight. Duncan, generally a solar figure, is the light that will not see the morrow, and that the morrow will not see.

The archetypal crime against the healthy progress of night and day for the Renaissance was also the archetypal crime of filial ambition: Phaethon's disastrous usurpation of Phoebus' solar chariot. Phaethon's premature seizure of his father's place neatly conflated two sorts of rebellion: the attempt to unseat the sun-king, and the Oedipal attempt to take the father's mount, against his strictest prohibition and before developing the abilities to manage or even survive the attempt. The story's moral is clear enough, and Shakespeare alludes to it to moralize his own cautionary tale: such ambitions, whether they are the seditious ones of a subject or the sexual ones of a son, threaten the universal order by which humanity survives, and the rebel must be sacrificed to preserve that order. After Duncan is murdered, Rosse reports that the royal horses "turn'd wild in nature, broke their stalls, flung out, / Contending 'gainst obedience, as they would make / War with mankind" (2.4.16–18). Like Phoebus' horses, they mirror the unruliness of the son who has stolen their reins, and thereby threaten the entire human race. Lennox's report that "the night has been unruly" (2.3.54) may therefore suggest to us more than that disorderly events have occurred during the night-time hours: since Macbeth—one of "Night's black agents" (3.2.53)—has usurped the sun's royal chariot, darkness refuses to yield to day as the natural order dictates. In the speech preceding his comment on the unruly horses, Rosse remarks,

> By th' clock 'tis day,
> And yet dark night strangles the travelling lamp.
> Is't night's predominance, or the day's shame,
> That darkness does the face of earth entomb,
> When living light should kiss it?
> OLD MAN:          'Tis unnatural,
> Even like the deed that's done.
>
> (2.4.6–11)

Their association of the sun's misconduct with a regicide (and, they are soon told, a patricide) invites us to adduce Phaethon's archetypal crime, which unites and moralizes Macbeth's various violations of nature.

Banquo's literal and figurative resistance to the onset of darkness parallels his resistance to the temptations of regicide. As Duncan falls asleep in Macbeth's castle, Banquo notes uneasily the very blackness Macbeth and his wife eagerly invoke: "There's husbandry in heaven, / Their candles are all out" (2.1.4–5). He seems to echo this obser-vation shortly before he, too, is murdered. His offhand remark to Fleance that "it will be rain tonight" suggests that he sees a dark, blank sky. In the form of his torch, he tries to keep daylight alive against this darkness; he has, as he promised Macbeth, "become a borrower of the night / For a dark hour or twain" on his journey (3.1.26–27)—the opposite movement to Macbeth's rush to nightfall. Macbeth's murderous ambition, as Rosse's remark suggested, again "strangles the travelling lamp"—this time the travellers' torch rather than the travelling sun. Macbeth intends to snuff out the final light of the old order, and relatedly the final obstacle to his new identity as a royal patriarch, by killing Banquo and Fleance in another artificial darkness that hides the deadly hand from the conscientious eye:

> Come, seeling night,
> Scarf up the tender eye of pitiful day,
> And with thy bloody and invisible hand
> Cancel and tear to pieces that great bond
> Which keeps me pale! Light thickens, and the crow
> Makes wing to th' rooky wood;
> Good things of day begin to droop and drowse,
> Whiles night's black agents to their preys do rouse.
>
> (3.2.46–53)

Macbeth now seems to be working for night as much as night is working for him. Day will suffer in this assault precisely what the First Murderer reports that Banquo suffers: wounds that constitute "a death to nature" (3.4.27). Banquo and Fleance represent the final force of daylight, the last gleam of hope: as the murderers close in on them, one comments that "the west yet glimmers with some streaks of day" (3.3.5). As their knives come down on Banquo, they answer his prediction of rain with, "Let it come down!" (3.3.16), as if the rain blotting the starlight and the knives taking his life were the same "it." Like Othello, they put out the light, and then put out the light:

> THIRD MURDERER: Who did strike out the light?
> FIRST MURDERER:               Was't not the way?
>
> (3.3.19)

But it was not. Fleance, prophesied to be the source of a new royal succession, escapes because the murderers have followed Macbeth's self-benighting policy to its misguided extreme by striking out the torch. By completing the nightfall, Macbeth and his "black agents" invite the next day to begin. Macbeth had told those agents that Fleance, like his father, "must embrace the fate / Of that dark hour" (3.1.136–37). As so often in this play, the "double sense" of words returns to haunt Macbeth: the luminous father (3.3.14) and his son embrace the dark hour as dusk and dawn embrace midnight. In *Macbeth,* the generational cycle and the solar cycle are like two clock-faces with a single dial. The striking out of the final light, like the stroke of midnight, announces the start of a new cycle. Nature regenerates itself miraculously from this terrible moment of nullity, as when Macduff rises to life after the terrible pause between his mother's death and his own birth. From the dire stillness of no light or life at all, a new light and a new life emerge. Rosse tells Lady Macduff, "Things at the worst will cease, or else climb upward / To what they were before" (4.2.24–25); in *Macbeth,* the sun or son always rises up again—except within the Macbeth household, which made itself an enemy of such resurrection. Some time passes before the renewed forces make themselves felt, but from the moment of Fleance's escape, we sense that they own the future. Macduff can still ask rhetorically of his country, "When shalt thou see thy wholesome days again?"; but Scotland's new sun king provokes a compelling if vague answer: "The night is long that never finds the day" (4.3.105, 240). This aptly echoes the lesson Macbeth forgot: "Time and the hour run through the roughest day" (1.3.148). Macbeth's has become a "distemper'd cause," and only at his death can it be declared that "The time is free" (5.2.15, 5.9.21).

As soon as Banquo's light has been put out, Macbeth and his wife become stagnant in time and benighted at noon. Macbeth calls Banquo's ghost a "horrible shadow" which has "overcome us like a summer's cloud"; trying to recover his temporal bearings that same night, he asks his wife, "What is the night?" and she replies, "Almost at odds with morning, which is which" (3.4.105–26). Her somnambulism is also a confused battle between a day-action and a night-action, and though "she has light by her continually, 'tis her command" (5.1.22–23), it cannot bring back the previous day's sun, nor give her a place under the new one. As Lady Macbeth wanders through the night in futile pursuit of a previous day, Macbeth wanders into a series of undefined tomorrows. But he, too, finds that his crime against the regenerative cycles has compelled him to exchange life for a "brief candle" (5.5.23); his figurative exchange resembles her literal one, and both represent the fool's bargain involved in the creation of their unnatural royal selves. That bargain may be moralized as Montaigne moralizes the resort to garments: "like those who by artificial light extinguish the light of day, we have extinguished our own means by borrowed means."

When Birnam Wood springs up in Scotland's new dawn, a sort of heliotrope to the new generation's royal sun, Macbeth shrinks away from it: "I gin to be aweary of the sun" (5.5.48). Daytime itself, as he inadvertently willed it, becomes his oppressor, joins the war against him. Young Siward, part of that new generation, assures Malcolm at the battle that "the day almost itself professes yours, / And little is to do" (5.7.27–28). Siward may simply mean that Malcolm's forces have nearly "won the day," to use a common phrase. But the active phrasing suggests that daytime itself seems almost to fight on Malcolm's behalf in an alliance with regenerative nature that leaves little to be done by the actual military force. In *Richard III* Richmond was urged by the ghosts of Richard's enemies to "win the day," and shortly thereafter we learned that the sun itself was refusing to shine on Richard's army, literally foreshadowing his defeat (5.3.145; 276–87). The same pattern underscores the character of Macbeth's defeat. He battles Malcolm's sunlight forces as an agent of the "black, and midnight hags" (4.1.48), and as surely as the sun rises, his brief dark kingship falls.

If Macbeth's suppression of daylight is a symbol, a tactic, and a punishment of his usurpation, then so is his attack on sleep. Having foolishly trapped himself in an endless night, he compounds the error by wishing away night's regenerative aspect. Insomnia, as I have said, is a fitting concomitant of ambition in Shakespeare: Henry IV must strive constantly to remain above his hereditary level, whereas Falstaff, who has sunk about as low as a human being can in the chain of being, as if it were a hammock, sleeps deeply at the very moment he is threatened with arrest. In *Macbeth* the correspondence between wakefulness and ambition takes on a greater importance and complexity.

Though Macbeth and Banquo are kept awake on the murder night by the same ambitious fantasy, the differences are crucial. Macbeth remains awake to overcome his political limitations, the same insomnia Henry IV suffers; Banquo remains awake to overcome his moral limitations, precisely the insomnia Falstaff spares himself. The distinction between these two responses to temptation resembles the distinction by which Milton's Adam consoles Eve for her own dreams of disobedient aspiration toward the Father's power:

> Evil into the mind of God or Man
> May come and go, so unapprov'd, and leave
> No spot or blame behind: Which gives me hope
> That what in sleep thou didst abhor to dream,
> Waking thou never wilt consent to do.
>
> (*Paradise Lost*, 5, 117–21)

Banquo is such an innocent, telling Fleance:

> A heavy summons lies like lead upon me,
> And yet I would not sleep. Merciful powers,
> Restrain in me the cursed thoughts that nature
> Gives way to in repose!
>
> (2.1.6–9)

Ten lines later we learn that he "dreamt last night of the three Weird sisters." The bad dreams, here as in Hamlet's "bounded in a nutshell" speech (2.2.254–59), are the fantasies of patricide, regicide, and incest that seem to haunt the whole world. No sooner are Banquo's words out than a vast image out of *spiritus mundi* troubles his sight: his partner in the sinister prophecy, also walking late. Banquo, apparently returning from seeing Duncan safely to bed (2.1.12–15), with any regicidal fantasies newly repressed, encounters Macbeth as a Doppelgänger, a Second Coming of his evil impulses. Macbeth is the waking figure of the cursed dream Banquo would be having were he asleep; Banquo might remark, as Leontes does in *The Winter's Tale,* "Your actions are my dreams" (3.2.82).

The notion that Macbeth is like any of us, only doomed to live in a world where one's dreams and desires become reality, is clearly bolstered by this moment, where we see Banquo horrified by the appetitive dreams the witches have aroused in him, then see his alter ego, stirred by the same force, condemned to live those dreams. Macbeth is again a version of the rash wisher in fairy tales: dreams are generally wish-fulfillments that evade the judging and censoring faculties, faculties that remain alert in us and in Banquo, crying "Hold, hold!" while we watch Macbeth stalk his desires. Freud cites approvingly "the old saying of Plato that the good are those who content themselves with dreaming of what others, the wicked, actually do." Our identification with Banquo cannot completely reassure us about our moral worth because we are forced to realize how fine and even fortuitous the distinction is between Banquo's soul and Macbeth's. No one who has ever awakened with relief from a dream of evildoing should feel any easy superiority to Macbeth at this decisive moment in his fall.

Half-asleep from exhaustion, Banquo watches the beginning of his regicidal nightmares acted out by Macbeth, who is crossing the stage in the opposite direction. Macbeth then watches distantly his own predatory advance, as we often watch ourselves in dreams; he announces that "wicked dreams abuse / The curtain'd sleep" (2.1.50–51). Macbeth has somehow *become* Banquo's bad dream, and Duncan's sleep seems to be tortured at this same moment by that same nightmare, which is closing in on him as a reality. The three characters are fatally jumbled together, as are the waking and dreaming states of consciousness. One result is that, after the regicide, Macbeth becomes both its perpetrator and its victim in an endless half-waking nightmare. As in the tortured sleep of Henry IV, the memory of committing a regicide and the prospect of serving as king work together against one's peace of mind; indeed, as Richard III discovers before Bosworth Field, they combine into symbolically appropriate nightmares of self-slaughter, the internal civil war implicit in ambition. Richard, in fact, foreshadows Macbeth's problems in another, more intriguing way. His nightmares, too, become reality; his dreams of defeat in battle come true under a sky that has stubbornly refused to turn to day. In the waking hours, when actions have real consequences, he is trapped in a repetition of the previous night. Macbeth, having lived out Banquo's evil dreams and fulfilled Duncan's, finds the boundary disappearing for him as well, finds it impossible to escape his nightmare either by sleeping or by waking. Awake, he is visited by terrifying ghosts, moving forests, deceptive riddles, prophetic and symbolic visions—the sorts of things that most people encounter only in dreams. But his dreams seem to be only an extension of his waking deeds and his waking fears. He would rather disrupt the universe than have himself and his wife sleep

> In the affliction of these terrible dreams
> That shake us nightly. Better be with the dead,
> Whom we, to gain our peace, have sent to peace,
> Than on the torture of the mind to lie
> In restless ecstasy. Duncan is in his grave;
> After life's fitful fever he sleeps well.
> Treason has done his worst; nor steel, nor poison,
> Malice domestic, foreign levy, nothing,
> Can touch him further.
>
> (3.2.18–26)

For their purposes, in fact, Duncan sleeps too well. By breaking the cycle that would normally have awakened him, they have inherited and perpetuated the nightmares of regicide which Macbeth imagined were tormenting Duncan's final hour. The implication is that the fear of a traitor bearing steel or poison wrenches Macbeth from his own sleep these nights. When the now dangerous world comes pounding on Macbeth's door, he says, "Wake Duncan with thy knocking! I would thou couldst!" (2.2.71). He wants the solar sovereign to rise again, bringing the new day's sun with him, thereby rescuing Macbeth on two levels from his nightmarish situation by revealing that he merely dreamed his evil deed. But cyclical renewal is precisely what Macbeth unwittingly forfeited when he abused "the curtain'd sleep":

> The death of each day's life, sore labor's bath,
> Balm of hurt minds, great nature's second course,
> Chief nourisher in life's feast.
> LADY MACBETH:                              What do you mean?
> MACBETH: Still it cried, "Sleep no more?" to all the house;
> "Glamis hath murther'd sleep, and therefore Cawdor
> Shall sleep no more—Macbeth shall sleep no more."
>
> (2.2.35–40)

The voice consigns him to sleeplessness by the same set of names the Witches used to assign him to ambition. When he asks them for reassurance against Macduff, so he may "sleep in spite of thunder," their answer is immediate and ominous: thunder, and the apparition of "a Child crowned, with a tree in his hand" (s.d. at 4.1.86). The forces of generational and seasonal rebirth unite against his craving for rest—"the season of all natures," as Lady Macbeth all too aptly defines it.

Insomnia, like the other cyclical failures Macbeth and his wife cause, briefly afflicts all of Scotland. To restore "sleep to our nights," Macduff must leave his native body politic for England, "to wake Northumberland" (3.6.31–34); but no such cure is available for the nightmares and somnambulism that erode the bodies unnatural of the king and queen. The Doctor and the Waiting Gentlewoman "have two nights watch'd" to observe Lady Macbeth's "slumb'ry agitation," but are then free to tell each other "Good night" and flee to their own restful worlds. The Doctor calls it "a great perturbation in nature, to receive at once the benefit of sleep, and do the effects of watching," but we may suspect that Lady Macbeth's perturbation of nature has entailed the opposite, an appearance of sleep with none of its regenerative qualities (5.1.1–79). She is propelled through an endless night by a driving nostalgia for the moment before the ambitious crime that rendered her both literally and symbolically ineligible for rest. Her sleepwalking thus complements her handwashing: both represent a futile effort to erase the consequences of a deed that murdered sleep both in Duncan and in her.

Shakespeare portrays Macbeth's crimes, from first to last, as costly violations of the procreative cycle. Dr. Isadore Coriat, one of the play's first psychoanalytic critics, identifies the Witches who instigate these offenses as "erotic symbols, representing, although sexless, the emblems of the generative power in nature. In the 'hell broth' are condensed heterogeneous materials in which even on superficial analysis one can discern the sexual significance." But superficial analysis dismisses too easily the discordant aspects of that emblem. These bearded women provoke Macbeth to mix the sexual elements ruinously, as they provoked him to mix the elements of the other natural cycles that must be polarized to be regenerative: night with day, dreaming with waking, and fall with spring. Under their influence he misuses his generative powers in such a way that he undermines the hereditary order, rendering his sexuality as barren and distorted as their own.

The Oedipal crimes constitute a man's ultimate offense against his hereditary nature, and the most insidious mixture of the generational cycles, which must remain distinct to remain healthful. Since so much has been written about the Freudian implications of *Macbeth*, however, this chapter will examine only those aspects of the Oedipal situation that relate to ambitious revisions of identity. Macbeth conspires with the temptress to "do the deed" that will make him king, or remake him as king. Norman Holland outlines the standard psychoanalytic axioms about the play: "Macbeth acts the role of a son who replaces the authority of his father by force and substitutes himself. The motive for this father murder is Lady Macbeth, the 'demon woman' who creates the abyss between father and son." Since Gertrude is the prize of Claudius' crime, Hamlet holds her partly responsible for that crime; Richard III entraps the Lady Anne by a trickier version of the same deduction. Freud argues that the woman's passive role gradually became misinterpreted in "the lying poetic fancies of prehistoric times" until the mother became an active instigator. Lady Macbeth seems to offer herself as the sexual prize of Macbeth's regicide, and threatens to become the murderous mother rather than the seductive mother if he refuses the task (1.7.56–59).

But, from my point of view, the reading of the crime as essentially ambitious rather than essentially sexual squares better with the situations the psychoanalysts describe. What Lady Macbeth actually provokes in her husband is an ambitious deed; the analogy to the Oedipal situation may be a resonance rather than a primary but veiled meaning. In offering to become either the seductive mother or the murderous one, she is reminding him that it is in his own power to decide whether to create this new royal self or to destroy it in its infancy. His success in creating it will be a measure of his sexual capacity, but that sexual provocation remains at the distance of a metaphor, and is intimately linked to the goal of a new birth rather than to any goal of sensual gratification. Occam's Razor seems to cut against the traditional Freudian reading in this case. Sexuality is Lady Macbeth's means to an ambitious end in the play's superficial psychology, and it would be fitting for the same transaction to apply on the play's deep figurative level. If psychoanalytic critics argue that "Macbeth's killing of Duncan represents hatred and resentment of a fatherlike authority" and that "Lady Macbeth embodies or projects Macbeth's ambitious wish," as Holland summarizes it, then the tensions seem more applicable to the hazards of ambition than to the "family romance" as such. Duncan is not Macbeth's actual father, but plays the paternal role in limiting the legitimate range of Macbeth's aspiration; the play makes it clear that Duncan is not a restrictive authority except in holding his preeminence and in promising it to another heir before Macbeth. Lady Macbeth is not Macbeth's actual mother, but plays the maternal role in offering to "embody" an ambitious new self for him.

Several critics have suggested that the murder of Duncan is figuratively a rape, or that the murder is only the offspring, or the projection onto Duncan, of a sexual crime between Macbeth and his Lady. Rather than making either the violent or the sexual aspect of the "deed" merely a metaphor for the other, however, my thesis makes them mutually dependent: this is a rape with procreative purposes, and it entails ripping the hereditary body politic untimely from its haven in Duncan's body. (The revelation of Macduff's Caesarean origins is, in this sense, another example of Macbeth's crime functioning as a rash wish that unwittingly invites its own punishment.) But this sinister seduction turns out to be a dismal failure. One critic equates the spirits of drink that the Porter says inspire but hinder sexual activity with the spirits that appear to Macbeth as witches: for each man, "The spirits that seem to make him potent actually render him impotent." The sexual situation is again not merely parallel to the political situation, but intimately linked to it: the attempt to conceive a new self becomes instead a loss of the original birth, and the effort to seize sovereignty over the process of procreation and lineage is steadily revealed as a forfeiting of all pro-creative abilities and lineal aspirations. Macbeth is left with a "barren sceptre" (3.1.61): the ambitious abuse of his sexual powers has ruined those powers. His castration, like that of Oedipal sons, is the final result of indulged Oedipal impulses; his impotence, like that of fisher-kings in myth, leads necessarily to his expulsion from rule.

The phallic character of Macbeth's crime is clear enough, however one chooses to interpret it. Led by a dagger, he advances toward Duncan's bedchamber "with Tarquin's ravishing strides" (2.1.55). Newly convinced by his wife to assert his sexual manhood by this deed, to become the "serpent" striking up through the "innocent flower" (1.5.64–65), Macbeth claims to "bend up / Each corporal agent to this terrible feat" (1.7.79–80); and when conscientious fear renders him impotent to act, she says, "You do unbend your noble strength" (2.2.42). When she mocks him for lacking the "manhood" to finish that task, she chooses to call him "infirm of purpose" (2.2.49). The murder is described by everyone, including the perpe-trators, as a "deed" or "act"; but these euphemisms for the horror that "tongue nor heart cannot conceive nor name" (2.3.64–65) refer to sexual deeds or acts as often as murderous ones in Shakespeare. This convergence of the two acts suggests the mixed crime of Oedi-pus; since the direct result is the creation of an exalted but sinister Macbeth, it may refer to the aspect of the Oedipus story that focuses on pride and identity, rather than the aspect that focuses on sexual psychology for its own sake.

The regicide is not the first time Macbeth had violently "con-ceived" an exalted new self and hewed its Caesarean path to life through another's body. Scotland is conventionally described as a mother throughout *Macbeth,* and only a few lines into the play we see Macbeth emerge as her heroic child. Using his "brandish'd steel" to make himself "valor's minion," he "carv'd out his passage" to Macdonwald and "unseam'd him from the nave to th' chops." A "passage" was a standard term in Renaissance medicine for "the necke of this wombe" at the base of the uterus. Richard II uses the same term when he strives to "tear a passage through the flinty ribs / Of this hard world, my ragged prison walls" for his rebirth in "a generation of still-breeding thoughts" (5.5.6–21), and Shakespeare will use it again to describe Coriolanus' determination to chop "his passage" through "Rome gates," which (as I will argue) become the symbol of his mother's womb through which any viable rebirth must pass.

Macbeth's first rebirth, however, is a defense of Duncan's paternal privileges rather than an assault on them. Disdaining the sinister allure of the "rebel's whore" Fortune—a version of the Oedipal temptress—Macbeth and Banquo confirm their identities as "children and servants" to Duncan's throne (1.4.25). But once the prospect of creating heroic new identities with their swords has presented itself, the loyal soldiers become susceptible to the lure of the sinister Witches, who offer them a rebirth that evades rather than affirms their hereditary subordination. The witches are Jocasta-figures, avatars not only of the temptress-figure Lady Macbeth with whom they share a provocation and a sexual ambiguity, but also of that sinister temptress Fortune, with whom they share a name: etymologically as well as mythologically, "the three Weird Sisters" are the women of fortune. Furthermore, witches and midwives were strongly identified with each other in sixteenth-century England, particularly in accusations that midwives induced birth to give the child a soul, then consecrated that soul to Satan by ritualistically killing the infant before it could be baptized. The parallels between this accusation and the witches' instigation of Macbeth's rebirth, death, and damnation, are certainly speculative, but also intriguing. Once it becomes clear that his first rebirth has not granted Macbeth a place in the royal lineage, he determines to use the same figurative technique that made him Duncan's loyal son to become Duncan's rebellious son. As with Prince Hal, Shakespeare undoes the dreamwork of a boy's father-saving fantasy, revealing the latent father-killing fantasy that was lurking symmetrically behind it. The witches perform the same psychoanalytic function, for Macbeth and for us, encouraging him to recognize the inevitable Oedipal conflict arising from his role as Duncan's child and servant, and thereby to recognize the perverse psychological mechanism connecting his loyal deeds with his "horrible imaginings."

The witches' prophecy is what sets the play's tragic aspect in motion, and it does so by luring Macbeth away from the normal cycle of generation. The prophecy seems to announce an equitable distribution of glory to the two triumphant soldiers: rule to Macbeth and succession to Banquo. But, as Lucien Goldmann suggests, the tragic hero generally finds that his gods "speak to him in deceitful terms and from afar off, the oracles which he consults have two meanings, one apparent but false, the other hidden but true, the demands which the Gods make are contradictory, and the world is ambiguous and equivocal." The hidden truth in the riddling prophecy, arising from the fog of the "foul and fair" day on the heath, is that the two promised forms of glory are mutually exclusive. A cause-and-effect relationship lurks unrecognized in the witches' division of the spoils: since Macbeth will seize a paternal identity that does not belong to him hereditarily, he will be forbidden to father a lineal successor. The prophecy that confronts Macbeth is therefore an Oedipal prophecy—specifically, a warning about filial rebellion and the castration that avenges it—as Lévi-Strauss argues all riddles are. Such a riddle tempts man toward the fatal violation it describes, sends him in pursuit of self-destruction through a desperate and deluded attempt at self-preservation. The "paradoxical impression that Macbeth gives of being morally responsible for his own destuction even though he is so heavily fated to destroy himself that the lines of his destiny can be read by prophecy" may be partly resolved by recognizing the unwitting act of choice that invites his fated barrenness. His fatal error, like that of Oedipus, is a failure to notice the cautionary aspect of the prophecies affixed to the gloriously inciting aspect; the contrastingly cautious Banquo avoids that Oedipal (and figuratively castrating) mistake. Banquo, the acknowledged enemy of Macbeth's "genius" or generative force (3.1.48–69), may safely partake of the crown by growing into it through generation rather than transforming himself forcibly into a figure of royal stature. As Edward Forset wrote in the same year that Shakespeare wrote *Macbeth*, "when wee be disposed to alter any thing, we must let it grow by degrees, and not hast it on too suddenly." The flesh of Banquo's flesh eventually grows into the kingly robes that hang so loosely on Macbeth's artificial person.

Lady Macbeth is quicker than her husband to recognize that murdering Duncan will entail murdering the procreative order. The fisher-king Duncan basks in the natural fecundity that he half-perceives and half-creates in the couple's home. Banquo explains Duncan's enjoyment of this castle in suggestive terms:

> This guest of summer,
> The temple-haunting martlet, does approve,
> By his lov'd mansionry, that the heaven's breath

> Smells wooingly here; no jutty, frieze,
> Buttress, nor coign of vantage, but this bird
> Hath made his pendant bed and procreant cradle.
> Where they most breed and haunt, I have observ'd
> The air is delicate.
>
> (1.6.3–10)

Just as Lady Macbeth has already begun replacing this martlet with a raven, and the domesticated jutties with battlements (1.5.38–40), so has she begun to replace this nurturant sexuality with its antithesis. Her plea that the spirits "unsex me," according to a recent study, contains a specific request that her menstrual cycle be intermitted:

> Make thick my blood,
> Stop up th' access and passage to remorse,
> That no compunctious visitings of nature
> Shake my fell purpose.
>
> (1.5.43–46)

Even her request that the spirits "take my milk for gall" suggests that the reborn Macbeth (like the reborn Coriolanus) can be nurtured into life only by fluids opposite to "the milk of human kindness" by which he was originally formed and fed (1.5.48, 17).

Freud understood this couple's loss of progeny as essentially such a rash wish, a barren instruction returning to plague the inventors: "It would be a perfect example of poetic justice in the manner of the talion if the childlessness of Macbeth and the barrenness of his Lady were the punishment for their crimes against the sanctity of geniture." The inconsistencies concerning Lady Macbeth's children, despite L. C. Knights's famous argument, actually makes Freud's point all the more convincing. If the children were concretely presented to us, Shakespeare would be obliged to provide a literal cause for their parents' poetically just lack of an heir. That would likely both alter the polarity of our sympathies and conceal the important symbolic cause behind a crudely physical efficient cause. This is opportunism on Shakespeare's part of the sort Knights describes, where the play works as something other than a realistic story, but if (as Knights urges) we ignore the apparent disappearance of the children, if we refuse to think of Lady Macbeth as a procreative creature, then we lose the moral import of that disappearance. Macduff's reasons for abandoning his family to slaughter remain somewhat unclear, perhaps for same didactic purpose. By including only the comment that this Caesarean figure "wants the natural touch" (4.2.9), Shakespeare suggests that the products of disordered procreation are deprived of heirs by a jealous natural order. Since it requires Duncan's death, Macbeth's royal rebirth thriftlessly ravins up his own life's means (2.4.28–29); since Caesarean operations were virtually always fatal to the mother in the Renaissance, Macduff's birth entails the same unwitting offense. By refusing us a complete factual explanation for either man's loss of progeny, Shakespeare focuses our attention on the defect they share and the nemesis it provokes.

This shared unnaturalness and childlessness enables Macduff to cure the disease that threatens the nation's procreative health. Macbeth's crimes against Malcolm's "due of birth" and against "nature's germains" in general have blighted Scotland's fertility (3.6.25; 4.1.59). The threatened kingdom is, as Macduff says, truly a threatened "birthdom" (4.3.4). In reply, Malcolm portrays himself as merely another agent of that blight, a creature of indiscriminate lust in conceiving children, and hardly better than Lady Macbeth in nursing them thereafter: he will "pour the sweet milk of concord into hell" (4.3.98). This causes Macduff to wonder whether there can be any hope for Scotland's regeneration,

> Since that the truest issue of thy throne
> By his own interdiction stands accus'd
> And does blaspheme his breed? Thy royal father
> Was a most sainted king; the queen that bore thee,
> Oft'ner upon her knees than on her feet,
> Died every day she liv'd.
>
> (4.3.106–11)

What this speech emphasizes is generational continuity: Malcolm's royal virtues should follow from his hereditary rights, almost as if orderly succession were virtue itself. The quality Macduff eulogizes in Malcolm's mother is her daily exchange of death and life, a pattern associable with the regenerative virtues of sleep, "the death of each day's life" as it is called at the time of Duncan's murder (2.2.37). This figuratively posthumous mother merges with Macduff's literal one into the notion of Scotland as such a mother:

> Alas, poor country,
> Almost afraid to know itself! It cannot

> Be call'd our mother, but our grave; where nothing,
> But who knows nothing, is once seen to smile.
> (4.3.164–67)

Macbeth's Caesarean rebirth has infected the entire nation with his nullified and self-alienated condition, and precludes any more natural births in the future. "Cruel are the times when we are traitors, / And do not know ourselves," the choral Rosse tells Lady Macduff moments before she and her babes are slaughtered (4.2.18–19). Disruptions of succession converted individual mothers and the mother-country into tombs in *Richard III* (4.1.53; 4.4.138, 423) and *Richard II* (2.1.51, 83), and now the same transaction threatens Scotland's future.

But eventually Scotland, like Macduff, is rescued from the dead maternal womb and begins a new generation of life. Macduff's role as the spearhead of this vengeful revival becomes an emblem of the fact that Macbeth is destroyed by the unlineal, unnatural provenance of his own royal identity. Macbeth is able to achieve his bloody rebirth only by performing a regicide; Macduff is able to perform his regicide, according to the prophecies, only because of his Caesarean origins. Macduff is, in this sense, the fulfillment of Macbeth's foolish wish to replace natural succession with abrupt violence. Macbeth again resembles Richard III, in serving as the sacrifice by which his nation restores its damaged lineal health, and Macduff is a suitable blade-wielding hierophant. When a society must purge a sin that has injured its fertility, it generally sacrifices a figure onto whom all the sin is projected, often a temporary mock-king; the executioner is generally a liminal figure who partly reflects or partly contracts the victim's particular taint.

A group of paradoxically mighty infants resume the process of generation as Macbeth's enemies. From the corrupt jumble of nature's germains in the witches' cauldron arise miraculously two such symbols of procreation's determination to survive and destroy the barren tyrant. The crowned babe, suggesting the rightful heir Malcolm, and the bloody babe, suggesting the Caesarean child Macduff, represent several things on other levels: the inheriting children Macbeth cannot have, the potential heirs Macbeth has sought to kill, the Oedipal children who typically abuse the father who was himself an Oedipal criminal, and the wounded regenerative order as a whole. For Macbeth as for Richard III, the failure to eradicate all such heirs, and relatedly the failure to terminate all such cycles, generates a nemesis that returns to destroy him. As in Greek and Christian myths, at least one heir escapes the tyrant's defensive Slaughter of the Innocents, and the army that defeats Macbeth consists of "Siward's son, / And many unrough youths that even now / Protest their first of manhood" (5.2.9–11). Once again Macbeth has succeeded only in interrupting a cycle he sought to override completely, and when it resumes he finds himself trapped in an unnatural generational isolation (5.3.24–26), with no child of his own to succeed him.

Macbeth is not only the bad ruler of Freudian myth, who deprives others such as Macduff and Banquo of their reproductive rights; he is also the bad ruler of fisher-king myths, whose own reproductive impotence causes his nation's crops to fail. The repression and vengeful return of human generation in the play is closely paralleled by a repression and return of the seasonal forces of vegetative life. The parallel has several revealing precedents:

> The first religious poet of Greece, Hesiod . . . tells us that when men do justice [their crops flourish and] "their wives bear children that are like their parents." So, on the other hand, when a sin has been committed—such as the unconscious incest of Oedipus—all Nature is poisoned by the offence of man. The land of Thebes "Wasteth in the fruitless buds of earth, / In parchèd herds, and travail without birth / Of dying women."

The Oedipal archetype, apparently from the very first, has been associated with a punitive collapse of nature's various regenerative cycles. In *2 Henry IV*, the haunted country is England rather than Thebes, but the ghosts are similar. Gloucester mentions "unfather'd heirs and loathly births of nature. / The seasons change their manners, as the year / Had found some months asleep and leap'd them over" (4.4.121–24). A few lines later, Prince Hal confirms the Oedipal character of this disturbance by stealing his sleeping father's unlineal crown. This blight began, according to the Gardener, when Richard II allowed the "prodigal weight" of "unruly children" to ruin a tree, and allowed "the noisome weeds" to "suck / The soil's fertility from wholesome flowers" (*Richard II*, 3.4.29–45). The natural order is only temporarily salvaged when Hal conquers France in deference to his forefathers, thereby acquiring a new world of vegetative and procreative fertility. The more lasting solution is the return of Richmond, who supposedly unites and renews the White and Red Roses.

The same correspondences appear in *Macbeth,* where the savior returns accompanied by his nation's foliage, and by young men determined "to dew the sovereign flower and drown the weeds" on their "march towards Birnam" (5.2.30–31). When Duncan arrives at Macbeth's castle, he is associated not only with the martlet's procreative aspects, but also with its role as a "guest of summer" (1.6.3). Conversely, Macbeth describes his usurping reign by adjacent metonymies that suggest vegetative and procreative sterility respectively: "Upon my head they plac'd a fruitless crown, / And put a barren sceptre in my gripe, / Thence to be wrench'd with an unlineal hand, / No son of mine succeeding" (3.1.60–63). He returns to the witches hoping for a revision of this prophecy, but the visions they conjure only serve to reinforce it. As early as 1746, John Upton perceived the brutally literal level of these portents:

> The armed head represents symbolically Macbeth's head cut off and brought to Malcolm by Macduff. The bloody child is Macduff untimely ripp'd from his mother's womb. The child with a crown on his head, and a bough in his hand, is the royal Malcolm, who ordered his soldiers to hew them down a bough and bear it before them to Dunsinane.

Having been lured by the witches across the threshold from reality into a fairy tale where words and imagination have an absolute efficacy, Macbeth overlooks this literal level of the portents, as he and other rash wishers overlook the literal level of their wishes; "the letter kills," as theologians warned, and the literal components of these apparitions emerge to kill Macbeth. Of course the armed head "knows thy thought," if it is actually his own head; it is an "unknown power" only to the extent that his own conscientious imagination is (4.1.69). The bloody babe is so overdetermined as a symbol that it resists any careful reading. The child's bough is all too easily interpreted as a symbol of regenerative nature, the rightful heir's sceptre that will replace Macbeth's "fruitless" one.

Yet there is a level on which this symbolic reading of Malcolm's return remains valuable, because even the literal advance of Birnam's branches symbolizes the unified nature that engulfs its betrayer. Dunsinane Castle, as a prize of Macbeth's ambition, represents on one level all of man's futile stays against his moral limitations. It symbolizes for Shakespeare what Ozymandias' statue symbolized for Shelley, and the advancing branches are the equivalent of Shelley's centuries of sandstorms. In the form of Birnam Wood, the balance of nature springs back against the kingly enclave man has manufactured against it; the wood, on this level, represents the endlessly persistent forces that erode humanity's efforts to make the world conform to its desires and reflect its consciousness. To build the castle in the primeval forest, to establish human sovereignty, land was cleared; eventually nature will reforest that land. The fact that civilization rapidly deforested Scotland in the era of the historical Macbeth makes the symbolism all the more plausible and evocative. The camouflaged advance on Dunsinane provides an accelerated emblem for the futility of humanity's ambitious projects, an ethical lesson presented by a sort of time-lapse photography.

Several critics have commented that this advance resembles a Maying festival, in which the young people carry green branches to chase out the tyrannical winter. Such an association, however subliminal, would serve to reinforce our sense that we are witnessing nature's cyclical victory over its barren enemies. What I am suggesting is that Shakespeare has grounded his warning against ambition in a parable applicable to the entire history of human civilization, and not just to the cycle of any given year, just as the confrontation between Hal and the Lord Chief Justice in *2 Henry IV* is applicable to much more than the reformation of a single unruly son. Shakespeare thus reinforces the power of the specific confrontations, and at the same time reminds us of their universal relevance; the hazards of ambition are an essential component in human experience, all human experience.

The shift in the moral balance from the history plays to *Macbeth*—the shift that makes *Macbeth* a tragedy—is visible in the difference between these two primal confrontations. We may not be entirely delighted with Hal's submission to the Lord Chief Justice and his banishment of Falstaff, but we sense that it is a choice we have all made, and that it is finally not only compatible with our humanity, but necessary for its survival. But, inasmuch as Macbeth's ambition may represent the essential projects of humanity, the very essence of our identity as *homo faber*—the creature who shapes his environment, with words and other tools, to his desires—the destruction of Macbeth by that fated moving wood can please us as humane justice on only the most superficial level. Conventional goodness is victorious, but it defeats an evil that Shakespeare invites us to recognize as a plausible extension of the things that make us human, and its weapons are the instruments of our oppression as well as our salvation. Shakespeare may have suggested all the natural concomitants to the political hierarchy in the history plays to remind people of the deep sinfulness and foolishness of attempting to overthrow that hierarchy; he may simply have been dramatizing the Elizabethan propaganda typified by the passages quoted earlier from Hooker and from the "Exhortation Concerning Good Order." But at some point Shakespeare recognized the logical counterpart to the argument that rebellion can arise only from a failure to recognize the seamless and providential character of the world's order. To dislike anything about nature is to lose sight of the essential principle defending the sovereign's authority over the will of his individual subjects. If all levels of the established order are so intricately linked, then repercussions may travel upward from lesser violations of that order, as well as downward from greater ones. If political ambition entails a parallel distortion of every other natural system, then we are all implicated in an array of crimes including regicide by our casual individual resentment of some inconvenient bad weather, and by our imperative resistance as a species to the landscape and the climate, a resistance palpably evinced by our houses and garments.

The notion that human beings are necessarily ambitious has substantial precedents in Renaissance philosophy. Petrarch argues that the specific need for shelter and clothing authorizes humanity's more general aspirations to surpass its given condition. As opposed to the lower animals, who "are allotted whatever is given them at birth and no more," man's naked frailties indicate that God wants him to achieve and acquire "as much as he is able in his acute genius to attain by living and thinking." Similarly, to Bovillus, as Ernst Cassirer explains it,

> freedom simply means that man does not receive his being ready-made from nature, as do the other entities, nor does he, so to speak, get it as a permanent fief; but rather that he must acquire it, must *form* it through *virtus* and *ars* . . . If he falls prey to the vice of inertia—the medieval *acedia*— he can sink down to the level at which only naked existence remains to him . . . The man of nature, simple *homo,* must become the man of art.

In *Macbeth* Shakespeare gives us glimpses of the dark converse of this glorious art, the grand transformation. What if man's greatest and most characteristic quality is trapped in a world where it can express itself only as sin, or at least where its natural activity will be perceived and punished as a violation of natural law by a jealous paternal God? This was the belief of the Gnostics, who felt that some higher God had planted a spark of his own divinity in each person, but that we have been trapped into a natural world inimical to that divine essence by a lower and envious God-the-Father. To the Gnostics, according to Hans Jonas,

> It is almost by exaggeration that the divinity of cosmic order is turned into the opposite of divine. Order and law is the cosmos here too, but rigid and inimical order, tyrannical and evil law, devoid of meaning and goodness, alien to the purposes of man and to his inner essence, no object for his communication and affirmation.
>
> The blemish of nature lies not in any deficiency of order, but in the all too pervading completeness of it. Far from chaos, the creation of the demiurge, unenlightened as it is, is still a system of law. But cosmic law, once worshiped as the expression of a reason with which man's reason can communicate in the act of cognition, is now seen only in its aspect of compulsion which thwarts man's freedom.

The cosmic order thus appears in its aspect of *heimarmene,* a Fate morally congruent with Mosaic law and opposed to the human essence, rather than *pronoia,* a true Providence. From such a viewpoint, Macbeth's steadfast opposition to, and destruction by, a unified system of nature would mark him as a martyr rather than a sinner.

Even his diseases, from the Gnostic perspective, are the proper tactics for opposing the Archons (the gods who rule this world) rather than punishments imposed by those Archons; this is revisionistic history on a grand theological scale. Macbeth's abstention from procreation, and his intimately related program of "uprooting" the heirs of others, recalls part of the formula dying Gnostics recited to escape the Archons, a sort of perverse last confession: "I have not sown children to the Archon but have uprooted his roots." To the Gnostics, the Mosaic God's injunction to "be fruitful and multiply" was an evil trick designed to entrap more of the divine sparks in his labyrinth. Even Macbeth's murder of sleep in himself and in others squares with the Gnostic project of awakening humanity from a sleep imposed by the Archons through a soporific poison that made us passive to this world's evils and forgetful of our true, more exalted home. Ambition is equated with insomnia in Gnosticism as it is in Shakespeare, but for the Gnostics that would have been an endorsement rather than a condemnation. The Gnostic is saved, not damned, by the Call from the supernatural agency that answers to an inner potential, as the witches' call answers to Macbeth's prior ambitions.

There are also elements here of the family romance, and of the decomposition motif by which that romance expresses itself in fairy tales as well as in psychotic delusions: a Gnostic's ambitions, apparently rebellions against the Father, are actually justified as fulfillments of his true heritage from the lost higher Father who rules the greater realm. The genetic identity is an obstacle to fulfillment for the Gnostics, and not a truly divine dictation of identity. In Valentinian Gnosticism, the Oedipal archetype emerges when the mother conceals the truly divine spark from the lower God-the-Father, and tricks him into leaving it "implanted in the human soul and body, to be carried there as if in a womb until it had grown sufficiently to receive the Logos." This Mother carries within her the seed by which the son reconceives himself, and she hides him (as Zeus and Moses were hidden) to protect him from the father's jealous and fearful wrath until the boy is strong enough to rebel successfully and thus reunite with her. To this extent, the Oedipal components of Macbeth's crime correspond to the Gnostic program.

The world of Macbeth thus moves closer to the world of Marlowe's Faustus, whose effort to find something above the mundane that answers to his aspiring mind becomes mired in the limits of the physical universe. The lower God has taught us to perceive as Satanic the voices—Macbeth's Witches, Faustus' Mephistopheles—that urge us to fulfill the transcendent within us; he has also learned how to imitate the grandeur of such voices when he chooses, for the purpose of luring us more deeply into the worldly labyrinth. When the witches implicitly laugh at Macbeth's defeat, as when the gods silently laugh at the defeat of Coriolanus (5.3.183–85), we may easily and chillingly sense that a spiteful conspiracy has triumphed over the ambition that is intrinsic to our humanity. What makes this even more horrifying is the recognition that this conspiracy has triumphed in the name of a "nature" we had been taught to revere as our mother, and to believe functioned in perfect harmony with our needs.

Nevertheless, on the play's primary level, the return of Birnam Wood to Dunsinane serves the human good as well as the natural order. A virtuous new human generation accompanies these moving branches, and is protected by them. Malcolm restores to Scotland the same combination of blessings that the flower-strewing Perdita brings into the artificial winter of Sicilia, making her as welcome "As is the spring to th' earth" (5.1.152). Macbeth cannot embrace this renewed vegetation as Leontes does, because in this adult fairy tale nature returns not in forgiveness, as a gift, but in vengeance, as a weapon. When the cycle he has briefly suppressed resumes its natural flow, Macbeth is stranded outside it. Even while this new spring burgeons, he becomes the yellowed creature of autumn, and "ripe for shaking" (5.3.23; 4.3.238). As the Gardener remarks about Richard II, "He that hath suffered this disordered spring / Hath now himself met with the fall of leaf" (3.4.48–49).

Time, which Macbeth would not trust to bring the prophecies to fruition, thus becomes his enemy. For him, as for Tennyson's Tithonus, the fact that the cycles of days, seasons, and generations continue all around him only makes his own steady decay more painful. Macbeth finds himself on a linear course into winter, while his wife retreats into a ritualistic repetition of yesterdays, until he loses her entirely:

> She should have died hereafter;
> There would have been a time for such a word.
> To-morrow, and to-morrow, and to-morrow,
> Creeps in this petty pace from day to day,
> To the last syllable of recorded time;
> And all our yesterdays have lighted fools
> The way to dusty death. Out, out, brief candle!
> Life's but a walking shadow.
>
> (5.5.17–24)

With the loss of his wife, Macbeth's hopes for diurnal or generational renewal disappear. In this Shakespeare seems to be building on a Jacobean commonplace. Richard Brathwait's *The Prodigals Teares* suggests the same associations: "I know Lord, that the candle of the wicked . . . shalbe soone put out . . . his faire and fruitfull fieldes laid waste, his treasures rifled, his pastures with all his hierds dispersed, and his children utterly rooted out and extinguished." Nehemiah Rogers' prodigal-son tract provides a similar analogue to Macbeth's resigned conclusion that "life's but a walking shadow," asserting that any existence devoid of spiritual growth and regeneration is "but a shadow of life." Macbeth's phrase also alludes ominously, unwittingly, to his earlier characterization of Banquo's ghost as a "horrible shadow" (3.4.105). Both Banquo's shade and Birnam Wood return as the ghosts of the natural life his royal aspirations have murdered, and as the fathers of the natural renewal he has failed to kill.

Macbeth's resigned conclusion, however, becomes a literal as well as a figurative truth. This speech is closely bracketed by revelations about the movement of Birnam Wood. Specifically, less than forty lines before Macbeth dismisses life as a walking shadow, Malcolm tells his soldiers each to "hew him down a bough, / And bear't before him, thereby shall we shadow / The numbers of our host" (5.4.4–6). In its emblematic march on Dunsinane, in other words, life actually *is* a walking shadow. Malcolm's stratagem, Macbeth's verbal metaphor, and Shakespeare's visual emblem, all agree on that point. Macbeth has not foreseen either Malcolm's military tactic or Shakespeare's artistic device, but most important, he has again failed to perceive the literal as well as the figurative meaning of a phrase, a phrase that subsequently becomes all too prophetic. The world, like the Witches, palters with him in a double sense (5.8.20). His very resignation to the hollowness of life actually invites life's true power to rise up against him, in a bitterly ironic reshaping of his own metaphor; again Macbeth becomes the fairy-tale figure whose unenlightened words return to haunt him. This complicated play on the notion of the walking shadow recapitulates in small the tragedy's central transaction. Macbeth's lack of faith in the natural cycles led to the rash wish that deprived him of cyclical regeneration; here, his lack of faith in life leads to a rash observation that unwittingly invites his death at hands of Malcolm's forces.

Cut off from his natural roots, Macbeth becomes a lifeless head on a pike (5.8.26), while Malcolm, festooned with green branches, takes his place. A contemporary of Shakespeare proposes a similar fate for his own murderous, incestuous, and overreaching protagonist:

> God would not permit him to enjoy that wealth, which to
> purchase had made him violate the lawes both divine, and

> humane, and prophane the most Sacred bonds that are in nature; [but] he that just labours, and lawfull industries, gathers up any thing shall see his goods prosper like a tree planted neere the current of waters, which brings forth fruite in its season.

The wages of sin are death, and the reward for cancelling the bonds of nature is at best an absence of life.

Malcolm, nominated as the new fisher-king by the procreative order itself, promises to reward his loyalists and to undertake all the tasks "which would be newly planted with the time" (5.9.30–31). This represents a return to natural continuity, not only in the character of the metaphor he employs, but also in the history of that metaphor. He assumes his hereditary place while using the same figuration his father used at the start of the play to thank *his* loyalists. As nature is a metaphor for heredity in this play, so is it a hereditary metaphor. With the big war that made ambition virtue successfully concluded, Duncan told Macbeth,

> I have begun to plant thee, and will labor
> To make thee full of growing. Noble Banquo,
> That hast no less deserv'd, nor must be known
> No less to have done so, let me infold thee
> And hold thee to my heart.
> BANQUO:                            There if I grow,
> The harvest is your own.
>
> (1.4.28–33)

The Witches know better than the egalitarian Duncan: Banquo shall be "lesser than Macbeth, and greater" (1.3.65) when his grains grow and Macbeth's do not, and this exchange suggests the reasons for that distinction. By accepting Duncan's vegetative metaphor, Banquo acknowledges his dependence on Duncan's fertility, and thus becomes eligible for the role as "the root and father / Of many kings" that the Witches promised him (3.1.5–6). By agreeing to surrender his fruits to the throne, he reserves a place for his scions on the throne.

Macbeth, in contrast, describes his "duties" as Duncan's "children" rather than as Duncan's "harvest," as if he expected his Caesarean deeds to win him a place in the royal family (1.4.24–25). That expectation becomes more obvious a few lines later in his violent response to Duncan's naming of Malcolm as heir to the throne. Macbeth must pretend to accept what is duly planted with the time, while secretly undermining it as the traditionally parricidal serpent:

> LADY MACBETH:                To beguile the time,
>     Look like the time; bear welcome in your eye,
>     Your hand, your tongue; look like th' innocent
>         flower,
>     But be the serpent under't.
>
> (1.5.63–66)

Macbeth thus subverts the harvest Duncan promises. As soon as the regicide has been performed, the Porter, pretending to welcome the newly damned to hell, first hypothesizes his guest as "a farmer, that hang'd himself on th' expectation of plenty" (2.3.4–5). This paradoxical farmer destroyed himself because a healthy, orderly harvest and reseeding thwarted his selfish speculations: Macbeth's hope that the death of a royal line will legitimize his unnatural succession parallels the farmer's hope that scarcity will drive up the price of his hoarded grain. This correlation gains conviction from the similarly damning flaws of the Porter's other guests, who are all "caught out by overreaching themselves." So, of course, is Macbeth, whose ambition has converted the blessings of nature into a curse.

Macbeth's attack on Banquo, like his attack on Duncan, arises from the extension of the planting metaphor into generational continuity. Banquo confronts the Witches with characteristic confidence in the natural order:

> If you can look into the seeds of time,
> And say which grain will grow, and which will not,
> Speak then to me, who neither beg nor fear
> Your favors nor your hate.
>
> (1.3.58–61)

Moral philosophers from Pelagius to Pico to Ralegh to Iago have used the selective cultivation of seeds as a metaphor for the legitimate range of self-improvement, self-cultivation. Shakespeare, rather more conservative in his view of human aspiration, has Banquo leave not only the seeding, but also the choice of which seeds will grow, in the hands of God alone. He may therefore become "the root and father" of a new royal family tree (3.1.5). Macbeth has sacrificed his otherworldly hopes for worldly glory, only to find that he has no one to whom he may bequeath his costly acquisition; D'Amville, in

Tourneur's *The Atheist's Tragedy,* makes much the same complaint, after a similar set of violations (4.2.36–39). But Shakespeare manipulates the vegetative metaphors to make the unity of divine and natural rules more vivid. Macbeth specifically complains about ruining his soul "to make them kings—the seeds of Banquo kings!" (3.1.69), unaware that his primal violation of nature necessarily entailed a loss of succession as well as virtue. This fear of seedlings, plausibly a premonition of the attack on his castle by shoots from Birnam Wood, compels Macbeth to strike down Duncan and Banquo in the hope that their scions, Malcolm and Fleance, will then be destroyed. He has not reckoned, with the proverbial truth Ben Jonson expresses in his *Discoveries:* "Severity represseth a few, but it irritates more. The lopping of trees makes the boughes shoote out thicker."

Precisely that truth is driven home to Macbeth, on both the figurative and the literal levels, when Birnam Wood begins its advance. But until it does, Macbeth supposes himself secure, because he has again failed to connect a figurative level with a literal one. His confidence that he can uproot these family trees is based on a literal reading of the Witches' prophecy that he cannot be defeated until the trees of Birnam move, which he supposes is impossible:

> That will never be.
> Who can impress the forest, bid the tree
> Unfix his earth-bound root? Sweet bodements! good!
> Rebellious dead, rise never till the wood
> Of Birnan rise, and our high-plac'd Macbeth
> Shall live the lease of nature, pay his breath
> To time and mortal custom.
>
> (4.1.94–100)

Either roots can be extirpated or they cannot; but because a family tree is a metaphor and a Birnam tree is real, Macbeth characteristically fails to see the contradiction in his hopes. Having broken the lease of nature, he can hardly expect to enforce it in his own defense; time and mortal custom, which he sought to subdue to his will, subdue him instead. All that remains of Macbeth's natural foundation, all that grows to fill his oversized royal robes, is what he sees disturbing his wife's rest: "a rooted sorrow" (5.3.41). For her as for the barren women of the history plays, sorrow is the only thing that retains a regenerative basis. Macduff, too, was cut off at the root, but according to Rosse, he retained some feeling for "the fits o' th' season" (4.2.17), understood the principle of cyclical growth. Macbeth evidently does not: the plants he lops off inevitably send up new shoots, culminating in the forest that envelops his castle. At the end of the play the impotent fisher-king is a lifeless head on a wooden pole, like an old tree that has dropped no seedlings, disappearing one spring in the eternal forest, vengefully excluded by the regenerative cycles his ambition sought to suppress.

# Chronology

| | |
|---|---|
| 1564 | William Shakespeare born at Stratford-on-Avon to John Shakespeare, a butcher, and Mary Arden. He is baptized on April 26. |
| 1582 | Marries Anne Hathaway in November. |
| 1583 | Daughter Susanna born, baptized on May 26. |
| 1585 | Twins Hamnet and Judith born, baptized on February 2. |
| 1588–90 | Sometime during these years, Shakespeare goes to London, without family. |
| 1588–89 | First plays are performed in London. |
| 1590–92 | *The Comedy of Errors*, the three parts of *Henry VI*. |
| 1593–94 | Publication of *Venus and Adonis* and *The Rape of Lucrece*, both dedicated to the Earl of Southampton. Shakespeare becomes a sharer in the Lord Chamberlain's company of actors. *The Taming of the Shrew, Two Gentlemen of Verona, Richard III*. |
| 1595–97 | *Romeo and Juliet, Richard II, King John, A Midsummer Night's Dream, Love's Labor's Lost*. |
| 1596 | Son Hamnet dies. Grant of arms to father. |
| 1597 | *The Merchant of Venice, Henry IV, Part 1*. Purchases New Place in Stratford. |
| 1598–1600 | *Henry IV, Part 2, As You Like It, Much Ado about Nothing, Twelfth Night, The Merry Wives of Windsor, Henry V,* and *Julius Caesar*. Moves his company to the new Globe Theatre. |
| 1601 | *Hamlet*. Shakespeare's father dies, buried on September 8. |

| 1603 | Death of Queen Elizabeth; James VI of Scotland becomes James I of England; Shakespeare's company becomes the King's Men. |
| 1603–4 | *All's Well That Ends Well, Measure for Measure, Othello.* |
| 1605–6 | *King Lear, Macbeth.* |
| 1607 | Marriage of daughter Susanna on June 5. |
| 1607–8 | *Timon of Athens, Antony and Cleopatra, Pericles.* |
| 1608 | Shakespeare's mother dies; buried on September 9. |
| 1609 | *Cymbeline,* publication of sonnets. Shakespeare's company purchases Blackfriars Theatre. |
| 1610–11 | *The Winter's Tale, The Tempest.* Shakespeare retires to Stratford. |
| 1616 | Marriage of daughter Judith on February 10. William Shakespeare dies at Stratford on April 23. |
| 1623 | Publication of the Folio edition of Shakespeare's plays. |

# Contributors

HAROLD BLOOM, Sterling Professor of the Humanities at Yale University, is the author of *The Anxiety of Influence, Poetry and Repression,* and many other volumes of literary criticism. His forthcoming study, *Freud: Transference and Authority,* attempts a full-scale reading of all of Freud's major writings. A MacArthur Prize Fellow, he is general editor of five series of literary criticism published by Chelsea House. During 1987–88, he was appointed Charles Eliot Norton Professor of Poetry at Harvard University.

HAROLD C. GODDARD was Head of the Department of English at Swarthmore College from 1909 to 1946. He is most remembered for *The Meaning of Shakespeare* and for his writings upon American Transcendentalism.

L. C. KNIGHTS is Professor Emeritus of English at Cambridge University. Among his many works are "How Many Children Had Lady Macbeth: An Essay in Theory and Practice of Shakespeare Criticism," *An Approach to* Hamlet, *Some Shakespearean Themes,* and *Drama and Society in the Age of Jonson.*

MAYNARD MACK, JR., is Associate Professor of English at the University of Maryland, College Park. He is the author of *Killing the King.*

HOWARD FELPERIN is Professor of English at the University of Melbourne. His books include *Shakespearean Representation* and *Shakespearean Romance.*

HARRY LEVIN is Irving Babbitt Professor of Comparative Literature, Emeritus, at Harvard University. His books include *The Question of Hamlet, The Gates of Horn, The Overreacher: A Study of Christopher Marlowe,* and *Shakespeare and the Revolution of the Times.*

171

ROBERT N. WATSON is Assistant Professor of English at Harvard University. He wrote *Shakespeare and the Hazards of Ambition* and has done research on Jacobean and metaphysical poetry.

# Bibliography

Ansari, A. A. "Fools of Time in *Macbeth*." *The Aligarh Journal of English Studies* 2: 45–59.

Armstrong, William A. "Torch, Cauldron and Taper: Light and Darkness in *Macbeth*." In *Poetry and Drama, 1570–1700: Essays in Honour of Harold F. Brooks*, edited by Antony Coleman and Antony Hammond, 47–59. London: Methuen, 1981.

Asp, Carolyn. " 'Be bloody, bold and resolute': Tragic Action and Sexual Stereotyping in *Macbeth*." *Studies in Philology* 78, no. 2 (1981): 153–69.

Bedard, B. J. "The Thane of Glamis Had a Wife." *University of Dayton Review* 14, no. 1 (1979–80): 39–43.

Berger, Harry, Jr. "The Early Scenes of *Macbeth*: Preface to a New Interpretation." *ELH* 47 (1980): 1–31.

Berry, Wilkes, and Steven Gerson. "From Tree to Weed: Macbeth's Degeneration." *McNesse Review* 23 (1976–77): 21–24.

Birenbaum, Harvey. "Consciousness and Responsibility in *Macbeth*." *Mosaic* 15, no. 2 (1982): 17–32.

Black, James. "*Macbeth*: The Arming of the Hero." *English Studies in Canada* 3 (1977): 253–66.

Black, Michael. "Myth, Folklore and Character in Shakespeare and Racine." In *The Equilibrium of Wit: Essays of Odette de Mourgues*, edited by Peter Bayley and Dorothy Gabe Coleman, 166–75. Lexington, Ky.: French Forum, 1982.

Brashear, Lucy. " 'My dearest partner in greatness': A Reappraisal of Lady Macbeth." *Selected Papers from the West Virginia Shakespeare and Renaissance Association* 5: 14–24.

Brown, John Russell, ed. *Focus on* Macbeth. Boston: Routledge & Kegan Paul, 1982.

Bushnell, Rebecca Weld. "Oracular Silence in *Oedipus the King* and *Macbeth*." *Classical and Modern Literature: A Quarterly* 2, no. 4 (1982): 195–204.

Byles, Joan M. "Macbeth: Imagery of Destruction." *American Imago* 39, no. 2 (1982): 149–64.

Calderwood, James L. " 'More Than What You Were': Augmentation and Increase in *Macbeth*." *ELR* 14, no. 1 (1984): 70–82.

Carr, Stephen Leo, and Peggy A. Knapp. "Seeing through *Macbeth*." *PMLA* 96, no. 5 (1981): 837–47.

173

Cartelli, Thomas. "Banquo's Ghost: The Shared Vision." *Theatre Journal* 35, no. 3 (1983): 389–405.

Cheung, King-Kok. "Shakespeare and Kierkegaard: 'Dread' in *Macbeth*." *Shakespeare Quarterly* 35, no. 4 (1984): 430–39.

Daly, Peter M. "Of Macbeth, Martlets and Other 'Fowles of Heauen.' " *Mosaic* 12, no. 1 (1978): 23–46.

Davis, Derek Russell. "Hurt Minds." In *Focus on* Macbeth, edited by John Brown, 210–28. Boston: Routledge & Kegan Paul, 1982.

Doran, Madeleine. "The *Macbeth* Music." *Shakespeare Studies* 16 (1983): 153–73.

Egan, Joseph J. " 'Of Kernes and Gallowglasses': An Error in *Macbeth*." *English Language Notes* 15 (1977): 167–71.

Egan, Robert. "His Hour upon the Stage: Role-Playing in *Macbeth*." *The Centennial Review* 22 (1978): 327–45.

Ferrucci, Franco. *The Poetics of Disguise: The Autobiography of the Work in Homer, Dante, and Shakespeare.* Translated by Ann Dunnigan. Ithaca, N.Y.: Cornell University Press, 1980.

Fleissner, Robert F. " 'The Secret'st Man of Blood': Foreshadowings of *Macbeth* in *Arden of Feversham*." *University of Dayton Review* 14, no. 1 (1979–80): 7–14

Fox, Alice. "How Many Pregnancies Had Lady Macbeth?" *University of Dayton Review* 14, no. 1 (1979–80): 33–37.

———. "Obstetrics and Gynecology in *Macbeth*." *Shakespeare Studies* 12 (1973): 127–41.

Gent, Lucy. "The Self-Cozening Eye." *Review of English Studies* 34, no. 136 (1983): 419–28.

Gorfain, Phyllis. "Riddles and Tragic Structure in *Macbeth*." *Mississippi Folklore Register* 10 (1976): 187–209.

Green, William. "Reinterpreting *Macbeth* through the Director's Employment of Non-Verbal Devices." *Maske und Kothurn: Internationale Beitrage zur Theaterwissenschaft* 29 (1983): 160–67.

Greene, James J. "*Macbeth*: Masculinity as Murder." *American Imago* 41, no. 2 (1984): 155–80.

Grenander, M. E. "*Macbeth* IV.i.44–45 and Convulsive Ergotism." *English Language Notes* 15 (1977): 102–3.

Hartnett, Edith. "Look, How Our Partner's Rapt." *Rivista di Letterature Moderne e Comparate* 30 (1977): 105–20.

Hawkes, Terence, ed. & introd. *Twentieth Century Interpretations of* Macbeth: *A Collection of Critical Essays*. Englewood Cliffs, N.J.: Prentice-Hall, 1977.

Hogan, Patrick Colm. "*Macbeth*: Authority and Progenitorship." *American Imago* 40, no. 4 (Winter 1983): 385–95.

Horwich, Richard. "Integrity in *Macbeth*: The Search for the 'Single State of Man.' " *Shakespeare Quarterly* 29 (1978): 365–73.

Hughes, Alan. "Lady Macbeth: A Fiend Indeed?" *Southern Review* 11 (1978): 107–12.

Jacobson, Howard. "*Macbeth*, I.vii.7–10." *Shakespeare Quarterly* 35, no. 3 (1984): 321–22.

Jaech, Sharon L. Jansen. "Political Prophecy and Macbeth's 'Sweet Bodements.' " *Shakespeare Quarterly* 34, no. 3 (1983): 290–97.

Jorgensen, Paul A. *Our Naked Frailties: Sensational Art and Meaning in Macbeth*. Berkeley: University of California Press, 1971.

Kimbrough, Robert. "Macbeth: The Prisoner of Gender." *Shakespeare Studies* 16 (1983): 175–90.

Kirsch, Arthur. "Macbeth's Suicide." *ELH* 51, no. 2 (1984): 269–96.

Kozikowski, Stanley J. "The Gowrie Conspiracy against James VI: A New Source for Shakespeare's *Macbeth*." *Shakespeare Studies* 13 (1974): 197–212.

Krook, Dorothea. "The Naked New-Born Babe Again: Perhaps an Art Image." *Critical Quarterly* 21, no. 3 (1979): 46–47.

Lambert, Jose. "How Emile Deschamps Translated Shakespeare's *Macbeth*, or Theatre System and Translational System in French Literature (1800–1850)." *Dispositio* 7, nos. 19–21 (1982): 53–61.

Lancashire, Anne. "The Emblematic Castle in Shakespeare and Middleton." In *Mirror up to Shakespeare: Essays in Honour of G. R. Hibbard*, edited by J. C. Gray, 223–41. Toronto: University of Toronto Press, 1984.

Leggatt, Alexander. "*Macbeth* and the Last Plays." In *Mirror up to Shakespeare: Essays in Honour of G. R. Hibbard*, edited by J. C. Gray, 189–207. Toronto: University of Toronto Press, 1984.

Levin, Harry. "Two Scenes from *Macbeth*." In *Shakespeare's Craft: Eight Lectures*, edited and introduction by Philip H. Highfill, 48–68. Carbondale: Southern Illinois University Press for George Washington University, 1982.

Lordi, Robert J. "Macbeth and His 'dearest partner of greatness,' Lady Macbeth." *The Upstart Crow* 4 (1982): 94–106.

Low, Lisa. "Ridding Ourselves of *Macbeth*." *Massachusetts Review* 24, no. 4 (1983): 826–37.

Lyle, E. B. "The 'Twofold Balls and Treble Scepters' in *Macbeth*." *Shakespeare Quarterly* 28 (1977): 516–19.

Marsh, Derick. "*Macbeth*: Easy Questions, Difficult Answers." *Sydney Studies in English* 8 (1982–83): 3–15.

McDermott, Dana Sue. "The Void in *Macbeth*: A Symbolic Design." In *Drama and Symbolism*, edited by James Redmond, 113–25. Cambridge: Cambridge University Press, 1982.

Mellamphy, Ninian. "The Ironic Catastrophe in *Macbeth*." *Ariel* 11, no. 4 (1980): 3–19.

———. "Macbeth's Visionary Dagger: Hallucination or Revelation?" *English Studies in Canada* 4 (1978): 379–92.

Moro, Bernard, and Willems, Michele. "Death and Rebirth in *Macbeth* and *The Winter's Tale*." *Cahiers Elisabéthains* 21 (1982): 35–48.

Muir, Kenneth, and Edwards, Philip, eds. *Aspects of* Macbeth. Articles reprinted from *Shakespeare Survey*. Cambridge: Cambridge University Press, 1982.

Mullaney, Steven. "Lying Like Truth: Riddle, Representation and Treason in Renaissance England." *ELH* 47 (1980): 32–47.

Nosworthy, James M. "*Macbeth, Doctor Faustus*, and the Juggling Fiends." In *Mirror up to Shakespeare: Essays in Honour of G. R. Hibbard*, edited by J. C. Gray, 208–22. Toronto: University of Toronto Press, 1984.

O'Brien, Ellen J. "Inside Shakespeare: Using Performance Techniques to Achieve Traditional Goals." *Shakespeare Quarterly* 35, no. 5 (1984): 621–31.

Paris, Bernard J. "Bargains with Fate: The Case of Macbeth." *American Journal of Psychoanalysis* 42, no. 1 (1982): 7–20.

Parry, Graham. "A Theological Reading in *Macbeth*." *Caliban* 21 (1984): 133–40.

Paul, Henry N. *The Royal Play of Macbeth*. New York: Macmillan, 1950.

Petronella, Vincent F. "The Role of Macduff in *Macbeth*." *Etudes Anglaises* 32 (1979): 11–19.

Rosenberg, Marvin. *The Masks of Macbeth*. Berkeley: University of California Press, 1978.

Slater, Ann Pasternak. "Macbeth and the Terrors of the Night." *Essays in Criticism* 28 (1978): 112–28.

Treglown, Jeremy. "Shakespeare's *Macbeth*'s: Davenant, Verdi, Stoppard and the Question of Theatrical Text." *English* 29 (1980): 95–113.

Tyson, Edith Slosson. "Shakespeare's *Macbeth* and Dante's *Inferno:* A Comparison of the Images of Hell, Damnation and Corruption." *Iowa State Journal of Research* 54: 461–68.

Usmani, Z. A. "The Drama of Values in *Macbeth*." *The Aligarh Journal of English Studies* 3: 63–79.

Waldock, A. J. A. "*Macbeth*." *Sydney Studies in English* 9 (1983–84): 3–20.

Walker, Roy. *The Time Is Free: A Study of Macbeth*. London: Andrew Oakers, Ltd., 1978.

Watkins, Ronald, and Lemmon, Jeremy. *In Shakespeare's Playhouse: Macbeth*. Newton Abbot, Devon: David & Charles Holdings Ltd., 1979.

Wexman, Virginia Wright. "*Macbeth* and Polanski's Theme of Regression." *University of Dayton Review* 14, no. 1 (1979–80): 85–88.

Williams, Raymond. "Monologue in *Macbeth*." In *Teaching the Text,* edited by Susanne Kappeler and Norman Bryson, 180–202. London: Routledge & Kegan Paul, 1983.

Wilson, Robert F., Jr. "Fearful Punning: The Name Game in *Macbeth*." *Cahiers Elisabéthains* 15 (1979): 29–34.

———. "Macbeth the Player King: The Banquet Scene as Frustrated Play within the Play." *Shakespeare-Jahrbuch* 114 (1978): 107–14.

Wolterstorff, Nicholas. "Was Macduff of Woman Born? The Ontology of Character." *Notre Dame English Journal* 12: 123–39.

Zeifman, Hersh. "*Macbeth*." *Theatre Research International* 4 (1978): 41–44.

# Acknowledgments

"*Macbeth*" by Harold C. Goddard from *The Meaning of Shakespeare* by Harold C. Goddard, © 1951 by the University of Chicago. Reprinted by permission of the University of Chicago Press.

"*Macbeth:* A Lust for Power" (originally entitled "*Macbeth*") by L. C. Knights from *Some Shakespearean Themes* by L. C. Knights, © 1959 by L. C. Knights. Reprinted by permission of Stanford University Press.

"The Voice in the Sword" by Maynard Mack, Jr. from *Killing the King* by Maynard Mack, Jr., © 1973 by Yale University. Reprinted by permission of Yale University Press.

"A Painted Devil: *Macbeth*" by Howard Felperin from *Shakespearean Representation: Mimesis and Modernity in Elizabethan Tragedy* by Howard Felperin, © 1977 by Princeton University Press. Reprinted by permission of Princeton University Press.

"Two Scenes from *Macbeth*" by Harry Levin from *Shakespeare's Craft: Eight Lectures,* edited by Philip H. Highfill, Jr., © 1982 by the George Washington University. Reprinted by permission.

"'Thriftless Ambition,' Foolish Wishes, and the Tragedy of *Macbeth*" by Robert N. Watson from *Shakespeare and the Hazards of Ambition* by Robert N. Watson, © 1984 by the President and Fellows of Harvard College. Reprinted by permission of Harvard University Press, Cambridge, Massachusetts.

# Index